contents

about barbecuing   6

starters   10
dips   36

seafood   38
breads   72

poultry   74

lamb   102
pizza   132

beef & veal   134
marinades   170

pork   172

sausages & burgers   190
sauces   206

vegetables   208
fruit   224

salads   226
potatoes   238

glossary   240

index   244

about barbecuing

The backyard barbecue has come a long way from the days when Dad donned an apron and charred some sausages. Now the barbecue is an indispensable part of summer life – and with instant gas and electric barbecues, some people barbecue every single night. It's cleaner than cooking in the kitchen, uses fewer pans, and it feels healthy and relaxed standing on the balcony or terrace turning the prawns with your tongs while your partner makes the salad. And once it's over there's not much to do in the way of a clean up.

basting brush

bamboo skewers

disposable baking dish

fish grill

meat thermometer

gas fuse

fish slice

long-handled tongs

metal skewers

wire brush

long matches

oven mitt

choosing the barbecue

Barbecues come in two types: covered and uncovered. A covered barbecue is the most useful because you can use it as an oven with the cover closed or as a traditional barbecue with the cover open. Small covered barbecues can be used on a terrace or balcony. If you normally entertain on a large scale however, you'll probably need a large fixed barbecue. If your barbecue is only used for quickly-cooked steaks, chops, fish and sausages, a portable uncovered barbecue might be all you need.

covered barbecues

Also called kettle barbecues (the most well-known is the Weber) they can be powered by gas or charcoal. They have a domed lid with air vents top and bottom. Cold air passes up through the bottom vents, providing oxygen to keep the coals burning, and swirls around in the barbecue, giving the food its characteristic smoky flavour, then leaves through the top vents. It works in the same way as a convection oven, the heat is reflected off the lid giving you two sources of heat so you can cook whole birds, ham and roasts. Uncover the barbecue to cook steaks, sausages and chops.

fixed barbecues

These are constructions usually made of brick which are built in the backyard. Their disadvantage is that they can't be moved if it rains but their advantage is that you can build them as big as you like with flat plates, grills and food preparation areas. If you entertain a lot in your backyard, especially for big gatherings, a fixed barbecue is often your best bet. You can use wood or charcoal on fixed barbecues.

portable uncovered barbecues

From tiny Hibachis to big wagon barbecues, you can buy gas or charcoal-powered varieties. They are on castors for easy mobility and many come with grills and flat plates They also have side flaps for bench space, and often a shelf underneath for storage.

the fuel

Barbecues can be fuelled by wood, charcoal, gas or electricity. Wood requires pieces of various sizes, kindling and paper. Allow wood to char before cooking and never use treated wood on a barbecue. Move food away from extreme heat to prevent burning. Charcoal is made from hardwood or lumpwood. It lights quickly, burns with twice the heat of heat beads and smells cleaner. Heat beads or briquettes are made from ground charcoal, coal dust and starch. For direct cooking, one layer of charcoal should cover an area slightly larger than the food. For indirect cooking, use twice the depth of coals as they need to burn longer. Place charcoal or heat beads in a mound and insert two or three firelighters among them. Don't attempt to cook anything while the firelighters are burning or your food will taste of kerosene. Allow the coals to burn down until they're covered with grey ash (about 30 minutes), spread them out, then start cooking. To increase heat, tap coals with metal tongs to remove accumulated ash, push the coals closer together, then open all vents and add more charcoal. To lessen the heat, partially close the vents and push the coals further apart.

Gas or electric barbecues are faster and will heat up in about 15 minutes. Gas barbecues come with a gas bottle and electric barbecues require a nearby power source. Most models have heat controls and at least two burners so you can cook different foods simultaneously. They work by heating either Lava or ceramic rocks. Lava rocks can be removed, washed then dried in the sun before replacing them in the barbecue. Ceramic rocks are non-porous and contain lava rock. To clean, turn them upside-down and allow the gas burners to burn off any residue. Most gas barbecues have a slide-out draining tray which should be lined with foil and sprinkled evenly with fat absorber. Replace this, and the grease receptacle, regularly as accumulated fat and grease can cause flare-ups.

Fit a gasfuse between the cylinder bottle and the regulator to prevent gas leaks and possible disastrous explosions.

cleaning the barbecue

All barbecues should be cleaned after use. It's much easier to clean a still-warm barbecue than a cold food-encrusted one. A gas barbecue should be turned on to high and when the grill or plate begins to smoke, turn the gas off at the bottle (to prevent gas build-up in the hose), then at the controls. For all types of barbecues use a stiff wire brush and cold water (no detergent) to scrub the grill and plate. Lightly spray or brush the grill with light vegetable oil before putting it away, to prevent rusting.

If your barbecue can't be moved out of the rain, invest in a vinyl cover to protect it from rust.

Ash from wood or charcoal barbecues should be allowed to cool down, then it can be spread evenly over the garden. If you have a small garden and barbecue frequently, this will clearly not be a solution for long. Place the cooled ash in a plastic bag and discard.

setting up the barbecue

indirect heat

This is used in a covered barbecue. With gas, the food is placed in a preheated covered barbecue. The burners directly under the food are turned off while the side burners remain on. With a charcoal barbecue, metal bars hold two stacks of coals against the barbecue's sides leaving the centre of the barbecue rack empty. A disposable aluminium baking dish can be placed here for fat drips, if desired.

direct heat

This is the traditional method, where the food is placed on the barbecue grill or plate and cooked directly over the heat source. It is the best method for sausages, steaks, burgers and vegetables. A rotisserie may be used with direct cooking over low burners (gas) or with an enamel baking dish below the roast (charcoal) to minimise flare-ups. Food can also be wrapped in foil to protect it when using direct heat.

combination heat

If you have a covered barbecue you can use a combination of both methods. Thick steaks or pieces of chicken, for instance, can be seared first, using direct heat, then covered and cooked using indirect heat for more even cooking and juice retention.

smoking

Smoking is a cooking stye in which the flavours of the food are affected by the choice of wood used. Hickory and mesquite are the best known woods for smoking, but there are many different varieties available, such as applewood, tea tree, cherry, peach or banksia. Wood chips have to be soaked first in cold water so that they will smoulder slowly over the fire, rather than burn. For additonal flavours and scents, soak a variety of herbs and spices in the water along with the wood chips. Smoking is best suited to moderate-to-slow cooking. Instead of placing the soaked wood chips and herbs directly onto the open flame where they burn too rapidly, put them in a smoke box to combust slowly without causing flare-ups. During preheating, place the filled cast-iron smoke box over the heat source. When smoke appears from within the box, adjust the burners on a gas barbecue to low. If using a charcoal barbecue, place the smoke box directly under the food and use indirect heat. For the best results when smoking try not to interrupt cooking by frequently opening the lid for basting.

useful tips

herb flavours
When you prune your bay tree or rosemary bush, save the clippings and toss them on the fire before cooking. The flavours of the herbs will permeate the dish – excellent with meat, fish and vegetables.

preheating the barbecue
A gas barbecue should only take 10 to 15 minutes to heat up but a charcoal or wood fired barbecue might take up to 1 hour.

cooking fish in newspaper
This is a very good way to barbecue whole oily fish such as salmon. Stuff the cleaned fish with fresh herbs and slices of lemon, season with salt and pepper and rub the outside with a little olive oil. Wrap in lots of newspaper (a big section of a Saturday broadsheet) and tie securely with string. Thoroughly wet the newspaper and place it on the barbecue, turning once. It will take about 1 hour, depending on the weight of the fish. Make sure the fish is skinned before eating.

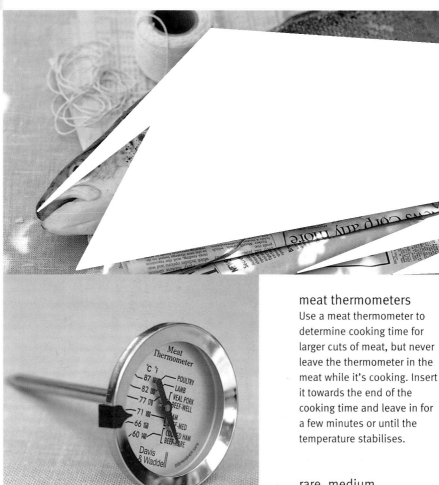

safety with barbecues
Always keep a spray bottle filled with water handy to douse flare-ups. It will not affect the food being cooked on gas barbecues but will cause ash to rise and settle on the food when cooking with wood or charcoal, so only use as a last resort in this case.

cooking times
These are to be used a guide only as the time can vary depending on the type of barbecue used.

meat thermometers
Use a meat thermometer to determine cooking time for larger cuts of meat, but never leave the thermometer in the meat while it's cooking. Insert it towards the end of the cooking time and leave in for a few minutes or until the temperature stabilises.

rare, medium and well-done
Try not to cut into a steak to see if it is ready – you'll lose juices that way. Instead, press the surface of the steak with tongs. Rare steak is soft to the touch; the outside is cooked and brown, the inside is red. Medium steak is firm to the touch, well browned on the outside and pink in the centre. Well-done steak is very firm to the touch, browned on the outside and evenly cooked through the centre, but not dry.

rare   medium   well done

starters

While they're waiting for the main event, keep your guests
happy with salt and pepper prawns, crisp, salty potato skins
dipped in sour cream or tender baby octopus – each one
is a great way to begin a summer barbecue feast.

oysters in bacon butter

PREPARATION TIME 10 MINUTES (plus refrigeration time) ■ COOKING TIME 10 MINUTES

**3 bacon rashers (210g),
   chopped finely**

125g soft butter

1 tablespoon tomato sauce

2 tablespoons worcestershire sauce

**2 tablespoons finely chopped fresh
   flat-leaf parsley**

24 oysters on the half shell

1 Cook bacon in medium frying pan until crisp. Drain on absorbent paper; cool.

2 Beat butter in small bowl; stir in sauces, parsley and bacon. Cover; refrigerate 3 hours or overnight.

3 Place a heaped teaspoon of butter mixture onto each oyster. Cook oysters on heated barbecue, uncovered, until butter melts.

makes 24

per oyster 5.3g fat; 259kJ

devilled squid with lime vinaigrette

PREPARATION TIME 30 MINUTES (plus marinating time) ■ COOKING TIME 10 MINUTES

1kg squid hoods

2 teaspoons finely grated lemon rind

¼ cup (60ml) lemon juice

1 tablespoon peanut oil

2 cloves garlic, crushed

2 teaspoons Tabasco sauce

2 tablespoons finely chopped fresh mint

LIME VINAIGRETTE

2 teaspoons sugar

2 tablespoons lime juice

2 cloves garlic, crushed

⅓ cup (80ml) peanut oil

2 green onions, chopped finely

2 fresh red thai chillies, sliced thinly

1 Cut along one side of squid; open out hoods. Cut squid into 1cm wide strips.

2 Combine rind, juice, oil, garlic and sauce in large bowl; add squid. Cover; refrigerate 3 hours or overnight.

3 Drain squid; discard marinade.

4 Thread squid onto 24 skewers. Cook squid on heated oiled barbecue until browned and cooked through.

5 Serve squid with lime vinaigrette; sprinkle with mint.

lime vinaigrette Combine ingredients in screw-top jar; shake well.

serves 8

per serving 13g fat; 878kJ

tip If using bamboo skewers, soak in water for at least 1 hour before using, to avoid scorching.

american-style pork spare ribs

PREPARATION TIME 15 MINUTES (plus marinating time)
COOKING TIME 10 MINUTES

1.5kg american-style pork spare ribs
1 cup (250ml) tomato juice
2 teaspoons grated lime rind
¼ cup (60ml) lime juice
2 tablespoons brown sugar
1 clove garlic, crushed
1 fresh red thai chilli, seeded, chopped finely

1 Cut rib racks into individual ribs.

2 Combine remaining ingredients in large bowl; add ribs. Cover; refrigerate 3 hours or overnight.

3 Drain ribs; discard marinade.

4 Cook ribs on heated oiled barbecue, uncovered, until browned and cooked through.

serves 8

per serving   16.8g fat; 1086kJ

moroccan-style lamb cutlets

PREPARATION TIME 10 MINUTES ■ COOKING TIME 10 MINUTES

Order french-trimmed lamb cutlets from your butcher. Moroccan seasoning is a dry-spice seasoning mixture available at supermarkets. Baba ghanoush is a Middle Eastern-style eggplant dip, also available at supermarkets or delicatessens.

24 french-trimmed lamb cutlets

¼ cup (40g) moroccan seasoning

green onion stems for garnish, optional

250g prepared baba ghanoush

2 teaspoons cumin seeds, toasted

1 Lightly coat lamb with seasoning. Cook lamb on heated oiled barbecue, uncovered, until browned both sides and cooked as desired.

2 Dip onion stems briefly into boiling water. Tie around cutlet bones; trim ends.

3 Top each lamb cutlet with a teaspoon of baba ghanoush and a few cumin seeds.

makes 24

per cutlet 5.7g fat; 394kJ

haloumi with capers

PREPARATION TIME 20 MINUTES ■ COOKING TIME 10 MINUTES

⅔ cup (160ml) olive oil

⅓ cup (55g) drained capers

600g haloumi cheese, sliced thickly

¼ cup (60ml) balsamic vinegar

2 cloves garlic, crushed

¼ cup finely shredded fresh basil

1 Heat 2 tablespoons of the oil on barbecue plate; cook capers, stirring, until crisp. Drain on absorbent paper.

2 Cook cheese on heated oiled barbecue plate, uncovered, until browned both sides.

3 Combine remaining oil, vinegar, garlic and basil in small bowl.

4 Drizzle cheese with dressing; sprinkle with capers. Serve with radicchio, if desired.

serves 4

per serving 62.1g fat; 2916kJ

potato skins

PREPARATION TIME 25 MINUTES
COOKING TIME 1 HOUR 20 MINUTES (plus cooling time)

5 medium potatoes (1kg)
2 tablespoons olive oil
2 teaspoons fine sea salt
1 teaspoon seasoned pepper
2 teaspoons finely chopped fresh rosemary
¼ cup (300g) sour cream

1 Scrub potatoes well; brush with half of the oil. Cook in covered barbecue, using indirect heat, following manufacturer's instructions, about 50 minutes or until tender; cool.

2 Cut each potato into six wedges; carefully scoop out flesh, leaving skins intact (reserve potato flesh for another use).

3 Place potato skins, skin-side up, in single layer on wire rack over disposable baking dish. Brush with remaining oil; sprinkle with combined salt, pepper and rosemary.

4 Cook in covered barbecue, using indirect heat, about 30 minutes or until crisp.

5 Serve hot with sour cream.

serves 4

per serving 38.3g fat; 1578kJ
tip Skins can be prepared a day ahead and refrigerated, covered.

basil prawns with avocado mash

PREPARATION TIME 30 MINUTES (plus marinating time) ■ COOKING TIME 10 MINUTES

1kg large uncooked prawns

½ cup coarsely chopped fresh basil

2 cloves garlic, crushed

1 tablespoon finely grated lime rind

AVOCADO MASH

2 medium avocados (500g)

2 tablespoons lime juice

2 medium tomatoes (380g), seeded, chopped finely

1 small red onion (100g), chopped finely

2 teaspoons ground cumin

2 tablespoons finely chopped fresh basil

2 fresh red thai chillies, seeded, chopped finely

1 Shell and devein prawns, leaving tails intact. Combine prawns, basil, garlic and rind in large bowl. Cover; refrigerate 3 hours or overnight.

2 Cook prawns on heated oiled barbecue, uncovered, until browned both sides and changed in colour.

3 Serve prawns with avocado mash and lime wedges, if desired.

avocado mash Mash flesh of one avocado, in small bowl, until almost smooth. Coarsely chop flesh of second avocado. Add to bowl of mashed avocado with remaining ingredients; mix well.

serves 4

per serving   20.8g fat; 1320kJ

lime and coriander octopus

PREPARATION TIME 20 MINUTES (plus marinating time) ■ COOKING TIME 10 MINUTES

Kecap manis, also known as ketjap manis, is a sweet, thick soy sauce available from some supermarkets and Asian food stores.

1.25kg baby octopus

2 tablespoons sweet chilli sauce

1 tablespoon kecap manis

¼ cup (60ml) fresh lime juice

2 cloves garlic, crushed

2 tablespoons coarsely chopped fresh coriander

2 limes, sliced thickly

1 Remove and discard heads and beaks from octopus; cut tentacles in half.

2 Combine chilli sauce, kecap manis, juice, garlic and coriander in large bowl; add octopus. Cover; refrigerate 3 hours or overnight.

3 Drain octopus; discard marinade.

4 Cook octopus and lime slices, in batches, on heated oiled barbecue, uncovered, until browned and cooked through.

5 Serve octopus with lime slices.

serves 4

per serving 3.5g fat; 967kJ

mussels with garlic butter

PREPARATION TIME 20 MINUTES (plus refrigeration time) ■ COOKING TIME 10 MINUTES

150g soft butter
3 cloves garlic, crushed
¼ cup coarsely chopped fresh flat-leaf parsley
2kg small black mussels

1 Beat butter, garlic and parsley in small bowl until well combined. Cover; refrigerate until required.

2 Scrub mussels; remove beards. Cook mussels, in batches, on heated oiled barbecue plate until mussels open. Discard any mussels that do not open.

3 Place a teaspoon of garlic butter into each shell; barbecue mussels until butter melts.

serves 10

per serving 13g fat; 601kJ
tip Garlic butter can be made 4 days ahead and is suitable to freeze.

salt and pepper prawns

PREPARATION TIME 20 MINUTES ■ COOKING TIME 10 MINUTES

Prawns can be peeled and skewered up to
6 hours ahead. Barbecue just before serving.

1kg large uncooked prawns
2 teaspoons sea salt
¼ teaspoon five-spice powder
½ teaspoon cracked black pepper

1 Peel and devein prawns, leaving tails intact. Thread one prawn onto each skewer lengthways.

2 Combine remaining ingredients in small bowl.

3 Cook prawns on heated oiled barbecue, uncovered, until browned all over and changed in colour; sprinkle with half of the salt mixture during cooking.

4 Serve prawns with remaining salt mixture.

serves 4

per serving   0.8g fat; 467kJ
tip   If using bamboo skewers, soak in water for at least 1 hour before using, to avoid scorching.

lamb kebabs with baba ghanoush

PREPARATION TIME 30 MINUTES ■ COOKING TIME 10 MINUTES

Baba ghanoush is a Middle Eastern-style eggplant dip, available at supermarkets and delicatessens.

1kg minced lamb

¼ cup coarsely chopped fresh flat-leaf parsley

2 tablespoons coarsely chopped fresh coriander

1 egg yolk

2 teaspoons ground cumin

1 teaspoon garam masala

½ teaspoon ground cinnamon

2 cloves garlic, crushed

200g prepared baba ghanoush

1 Using one hand, combine mince, parsley, coriander, egg yolk, spices and garlic in large bowl.

2 Roll tablespoons of mixture into oval shapes; shape two pieces of mince mixture onto each skewer.

3 Cook kebabs on heated oiled barbecue until browned all over and cooked as desired.

4 Serve kebabs with baba ghanoush.

serves 6

per serving 24g fat; 1571kJ

tip If using bamboo skewers, soak in water for at least 1 hour before using, to avoid scorching.

marinated chicken wings

PREPARATION TIME 20 MINUTES (plus marinating time)
COOKING TIME 40 MINUTES

1.5kg large chicken wings
1 cup (250ml) tomato sauce
½ cup (125ml) plum sauce
¼ cup (60ml) worcestershire sauce
¼ cup (50g) firmly packed brown sugar
2 cloves garlic, crushed

1 Cut chicken wings into three pieces at joints; discard tips.

2 Combine remaining ingredients in large bowl; add chicken. Cover; refrigerate 3 hours or overnight.

3 Drain chicken; discard marinade.

4 Place chicken on oiled wire rack over disposable baking dish. Cook in covered barbecue, using indirect heat, following manufacturer's instructions, about 40 minutes or until browned and cooked through.

serves 6

per serving 24.3g fat; 1961kJ

balsamic garlic octopus

PREPARATION TIME 20 MINUTES (plus marinating time) ■ COOKING TIME 10 MINUTES

1kg baby octopus

2 cloves garlic, crushed

⅓ cup (80ml) olive oil

⅓ cup (80ml) balsamic vinegar

**¼ cup coarsely chopped
    fresh oregano**

1 Clean heads; remove and discard beaks from octopus.

2 Combine garlic, oil, vinegar and oregano in large bowl; add octopus. Cover; refrigerate 3 hours or overnight.

3 Drain octopus; discard marinade.

4 Cook octopus on heated oiled barbecue, uncovered, until browned and cooked through.

serves 4

per serving 20.7g fat; 1387kJ

prawn kebabs with chilli lime sauce

PREPARATION TIME 40 MINUTES (plus marinating time) ■ COOKING TIME 25 MINUTES (plus cooling time)

1kg medium uncooked prawns

2 cloves garlic, crushed

1 tablespoon finely chopped fresh lemon grass

1 tablespoon balsamic vinegar

1 tablespoon coarsely chopped fresh coriander

1 tablespoon peanut oil

4 green onions

CHILLI LIME SAUCE

²/₃ cup (150g) sugar

¹/₂ cup (125ml) water

1 teaspoon finely grated lime rind

2 fresh red thai chillies, seeded, chopped finely

2 tablespoons sweet chilli sauce

¹/₃ cup (80ml) lime juice

1 Shell and devein prawns, leaving tails intact.

2 Combine garlic, lemon grass, vinegar, coriander and oil in large bowl; add prawns. Cover; refrigerate 3 hours or overnight.

3 Drain prawns; discard marinade.

4 Cut onions into 5cm lengths. Thread onion and prawns onto eight skewers.

5 Cook prawns on heated oiled barbecue, uncovered, until browned both sides and changed in colour.

6 Serve prawns with chilli lime sauce.

chilli lime sauce Combine sugar and the water in small saucepan; stir over heat, without boiling, until sugar dissolves. Simmer, uncovered, without stirring, 5 minutes. Add rind, chilli and sauce; simmer, uncovered, 5 minutes. Stir in juice; cool.

serves 4

per serving 5.7g fat; 1321kJ

tip If using bamboo skewers, soak in water for at least 1 hour before using, to avoid scorching.

glazed chicken sticks

PREPARATION TIME 35 MINUTES (plus marinating time) ■ COOKING TIME 10 MINUTES

1kg chicken wings
4 green onions, chopped finely
$1/2$ cup (125ml) green ginger wine
$1/4$ cup (60ml) light soy sauce
$1/4$ cup (60ml) dark soy sauce
1 tablespoon brown sugar

1 Cut chicken wings into three pieces at joints; discard tips. Holding small end of bone, trim around bone with sharp knife to cut meat free from bone. Cut, scrape and push meat down to large end (half of the pieces will have an extra fine bone that should be removed).

2 Using fingers, pull skin and meat down over end of bone; each piece will resemble a baby drumstick.

3 Combine onion, wine, sauces and sugar in large bowl; add chicken. Cover; refrigerate 3 hours or overnight.

4 Drain chicken; discard marinade.

5 Cook chicken on heated oiled barbecue, uncovered, until browned and cooked through.

serves 6

per serving 16g fat; 1078kJ
tip Recipe can be prepared a day ahead and is suitable to freeze.

garlic prawns

PREPARATION TIME 20 MINUTES ■ COOKING TIME 10 MINUTES

1kg large uncooked prawns

2 tablespoons olive oil

6 cloves garlic, crushed

2 fresh red thai chillies, seeded, chopped finely

2 teaspoons sea salt flakes

1 tablespoon finely chopped fresh flat-leaf parsley

1 Shell and devein prawns, leaving tails intact. Combine prawns with remaining ingredients in large bowl.

2 Cook prawns on heated oiled barbecue, uncovered, until browned both sides and changed in colour. Serve with mixed salad leaves, if desired.

serves 4

per serving   10g fat; 819kJ

chicken kebabs with coriander pesto

PREPARATION TIME 35 MINUTES (plus marinating time) ■ COOKING TIME 10 MINUTES

2 teaspoons finely grated lime rind

2 tablespoons lime juice

1 teaspoon ground coriander

1 tablespoon peanut oil

**700g chicken breast fillets,
chopped coarsely**

**¼ cup (35g) unsalted peanuts,
toasted, chopped coarsely**

CORIANDER PESTO

**2 tablespoons unsalted
peanuts, toasted**

**½ cup firmly packed fresh
coriander leaves**

2 cloves garlic, crushed

½ cup (125ml) peanut oil

1 Combine rind, juice, coriander and oil in large bowl; add chicken.
Cover; refrigerate 3 hours or overnight.

2 Drain chicken; discard marinade. Thread chicken onto 12 skewers.

3 Cook chicken on heated oiled barbecue, uncovered, until browned all over
and cooked through.

4 Serve chicken with coriander pesto; sprinkle with peanuts.

coriander pesto Blend or process ingredients until combined.

serves 6

per serving 33g fat; 1713kJ

tip If using bamboo skewers, soak in water for at least 1 hour before using, to avoid scorching.

black bean and chilli prawn kebabs

PREPARATION TIME 30 MINUTES (plus marinating time) ■ COOKING TIME 10 MINUTES

1kg medium uncooked prawns
$\frac{1}{2}$ cup (125ml) soy sauce
1$\frac{1}{2}$ tablespoons salted black beans, rinsed, chopped coarsely
1 clove garlic, crushed
2 teaspoons grated fresh ginger
1 tablespoon dry sherry
1 teaspoon sesame oil
1 fresh red thai chilli, seeded, chopped finely
1 fresh red thai chili, sliced thinly

1 Shell and devein prawns.

2 Combine 2 tablespoons of the sauce with beans, garlic, ginger, sherry, oil and chopped chilli in large bowl; add prawns. Cover; refrigerate 3 hours or overnight.

3 Drain prawns; discard marinade. Thread prawns onto 12 skewers.

4 Cook prawns on heated oiled barbecue until browned both sides and changed in colour.

5 Serve prawns with combined remaining sauce and sliced chilli.

makes 12

per kebab 0.8g fat; 208kJ
tip If using bamboo skewers, soak in water for at least 1 hour before using, to avoid scorching.

beetroot tzatziki

PREPARATION TIME 15 MINUTES
COOKING TIME 1 HOUR (plus cooling time)

2 large beetroot (400g)
1 cup (280g) yogurt
1/2 cup (100g) ricotta cheese
2 cloves garlic, crushed
2 tablespoons lemon juice
1/4 cup finely chopped fresh chives
1/4 cup finely chopped fresh mint

1 Place unpeeled beetroot in disposable baking dish. Cook in covered barbecue, using indirect heat, following manufacturer's instructions, about 1 hour or until tender; cool.

2 Peel beetroot; chop coarsely. Place beetroot in food processor; combine with yogurt, cheese, garlic and juice. Blend until combined.

3 Remove from processor; stir in herbs.

serves 6

per serving 3.6g fat; 362kJ
tip Wear a pair of rubber gloves when you handle the cooked beetroot to avoid staining your hands.

eggplant parsley dip

PREPARATION TIME 15 MINUTES (plus refrigeration time)
COOKING TIME 1 HOUR (plus cooling time)

1 large eggplant (500g)
1 medium white onion (150g), chopped finely
2 tablespoons yogurt
2 cloves garlic, crushed
1 tablespoon red wine vinegar
2 tablespoons olive oil
1/2 cup finely chopped fresh flat-leaf parsley

1 Prick eggplant all over with fork; place in disposable baking dish. Cook in covered barbecue, using indirect heat, following manufacturer's instructions, about 1 hour or until soft. When cool enough to handle, halve eggplant; scoop out flesh. Chop flesh coarsely; discard skin.

2 Blend or process eggplant with onion, yogurt, garlic, vinegar and oil; blend until chopped coarsely.

3 Add parsley; blend until just combined. Refrigerate until cold.

serves 6

per serving 6.6g fat; 348kJ

sweet chilli dip

PREPARATION TIME 5 MINUTES

250g softened cream cheese
$\frac{1}{4}$ cup (60ml) mild sweet chilli sauce
1 tablespoon finely chopped
   fresh coriander

1 Combine ingredients in small bowl.

2 Serve with grissini (breadsticks), crackers or vegetable sticks, if desired.

serves 4

per serving 21.1g fat; 954kJ

tomato salsa

PREPARATION TIME 15 MINUTES

3 medium tomatoes (570g), seeded,
   chopped finely
1 small avocado (200g), chopped finely
1 medium red onion (170g), chopped finely
2 fresh red thai chillies, seeded,
   chopped finely
2 tablespoons coarsely chopped
   fresh coriander
130g can corn kernels, rinsed, drained
1 tablespoon lemon juice

1 Combine ingredients in medium bowl.

2 Serve with corn chips or baked flour tortilla wedges, if desired.

serves 6

per serving 5.5g fat; 375kJ

dips

seafood

Barbecuing is the best way to cook seafood, the outdoor smoky flavours adding zest to the moist delicacy of fish and shellfish. It's also extraordinarily quick and easy – and all that fishy smell stays outside!

barramundi with yogurt and ginger

PREPARATION TIME 15 MINUTES ■ COOKING TIME 10 MINUTES

⅓ cup (95g) yogurt

1 teaspoon finely grated fresh ginger

½ teaspoon finely grated lime rind

1 tablespoon coarsely chopped fresh mint

1 tablespoon coarsely chopped fresh coriander

4 barramundi fillets (1kg)

2 tablespoons lime juice

1 lebanese cucumber (130g), grated coarsely

4 trimmed radishes (60g), grated coarsely

1 Combine yogurt, ginger, rind, mint and coriander in small bowl.

2 Cook fish on heated oiled barbecue, uncovered, until browned both sides and just cooked through.

3 Serve fish drizzled with juice. Top with combined cucumber and radish; drizzle with yogurt mixture.

serves 4

per serving 3.9g fat; 1114kJ

gemfish kebabs

PREPARATION TIME 20 MINUTES (plus marinating time) ■ COOKING TIME 50 MINUTES

You can use any firm white fish fillets for this recipe.

⅓ cup coarsely chopped fresh coriander leaves

2 teaspoons ground cumin

¼ teaspoon ground turmeric

1 clove garlic, quartered

1 fresh red thai chilli, seeded, chopped coarsely

1 tablespoon peanut oil

1 large red onion (300g), sliced thinly

500g gemfish fillets

1kg tiny new potatoes, halved

¼ cup (60ml) olive oil

1 tablespoon cumin seeds, crushed

2 teaspoons sea salt

250g baby spinach leaves

2 teaspoons lemon juice

2 teaspoons white wine vinegar

1 Blend or process ¼ cup of the coriander with cumin, turmeric, garlic, chilli, peanut oil and a quarter of the onion until smooth.

2 Cut fish into 2cm pieces. Combine fish with coriander mixture in medium bowl. Cover; refrigerate 3 hours or overnight.

3 Boil, steam or microwave potato until tender; drain. Toss hot potato with 1 tablespoon of the olive oil, cumin seeds, remaining onion and salt. Place in single layer in large baking dish. Bake, uncovered, in moderate oven about 40 minutes or until potato is browned and crisp; place in large bowl. Add spinach; toss gently to combine with potato.

4 Meanwhile, thread fish onto eight skewers. Cook fish, in batches, on heated oiled barbecue until browned and cooked through. Combine remaining coriander, remaining olive oil, juice and vinegar in screw-top jar; shake well.

5 Place potato mixture on serving plates; top with fish and dressing.

serves 4

per serving 21g fat; 1920kJ

tip If using bamboo skewers, soak in water for at least 1 hour before using, to avoid scorching.

tuna with olive salsa

PREPARATION TIME 15 MINUTES (plus marinating time)
COOKING TIME 10 MINUTES

6 tuna steaks (1kg)
½ cup (125ml) olive oil
¼ cup (60ml) lemon juice
2 cloves garlic, crushed
4 medium tomatoes (360g), quartered
50g baby spinach leaves

OLIVE SALSA
200g seeded kalamata olives, chopped finely
⅓ cup (50g) drained, coarsely chopped capers
2 tablespoons finely grated lemon rind
½ cup coarsely chopped fresh flat-leaf parsley
¼ cup coarsely chopped fresh oregano

1 Place tuna in shallow dish; pour over combined oil, juice and garlic. Cover; refrigerate 1 hour.

2 Drain tuna; discard marinade.

3 Cook tuna and tomato on heated oiled barbecue, uncovered, until tuna is browned both sides and cooked as desired, and tomato is tender.

4 Serve tuna with tomato, olive salsa and spinach.

olive salsa Combine ingredients in small bowl.

serves 6

per serving 22.2g fat; 1726kJ

lobster with lime and herbs

PREPARATION TIME 20 MINUTES (plus marinating time) ■ COOKING TIME 15 MINUTES

**6 medium uncooked
  lobster tails (2.2kg)**

⅓ cup (80ml) olive oil

2 teaspoons grated lime rind

½ cup (125ml) lime juice

2 cloves garlic, crushed

**2 tablespoons coarsely chopped
  fresh coriander**

**2 tablespoons coarsely chopped
  fresh flat-leaf parsley**

6 limes, cut into wedges

1 Remove and discard soft shell from underneath lobster tails to expose flesh.

2 Combine oil, rind, juice, garlic, coriander and parsley in large bowl;
add lobster. Cover; refrigerate 1 hour.

3 Drain lobster; reserve marinade.

4 Cook lobster on heated oiled barbecue, uncovered, until browned all over
and cooked through, brushing lobster occasionally with reserved marinade
during cooking. Serve with lime.

serves 6

per serving 15g fat; 1719kJ

coconut prawns with turmeric coriander mayonnaise

PREPARATION TIME 30 MINUTES ■ COOKING TIME 10 MINUTES

1kg large uncooked prawns

2 eggs, beaten lightly

1 cup (70g) shredded coconut

6 potato roti, to serve

**TURMERIC CORIANDER
MAYONNAISE**

¼ teaspoon ground turmeric

2 tablespoons boiling water

1 clove garlic, crushed

2 teaspoons finely grated lemon rind

½ cup (150g) mayonnaise

**2 tablespoons finely chopped
   fresh coriander**

1 Peel and devein prawns, leaving tails intact.

2 Dip prawns in egg; coat in coconut.

3 Cook prawns on heated oiled barbecue plate, uncovered, until browned and cooked through.

4 Cook roti on heated oiled barbecue, uncovered, until browned.

5 Serve prawns with turmeric coriander mayonnaise and roti.

turmeric coriander mayonnaise Combine ingredients in small bowl.

serves 4

per serving   27.6g fat; 2099kJ

lime-marinated cutlets
with tomato and onion salsa

PREPARATION TIME 20 MINUTES (plus marinating time) ■ COOKING TIME 10 MINUTES

1 clove garlic, crushed
1 tablespoon finely grated lime rind
2 tablespoons oyster sauce
½ cup (125ml) sweet chilli sauce
½ cup (125ml) lime juice
4 blue-eye cutlets (1kg)
2 medium tomatoes (380g), seeded, chopped finely
1 medium red onion (170g), chopped finely

1 Combine garlic, rind, oyster sauce and ⅓ cup each of the chilli sauce and juice in large bowl; add fish. Cover; refrigerate 1 hour.

2 Meanwhile, combine tomato, onion, remaining chilli sauce and remaining juice in small bowl. Cover; refrigerate until required.

3 Drain fish; reserve marinade.

4 Cook fish on heated oiled barbecue, uncovered, until browned both sides and just cooked through, brushing occasionally with reserved marinade during cooking.

5 Serve fish topped with tomato and onion salsa.

serves 4

per serving 6.3g fat; 1308kJ

squid with watercress salad

PREPARATION TIME 20 MINUTES (plus standing time) ■ COOKING TIME 10 MINUTES

1kg squid hoods

1½ teaspoons ground cumin

2 tablespoons finely chopped fresh dill

2 tablespoons lemon juice

2 tablespoons barbecue sauce

¼ cup (60ml) sweet chilli sauce

¼ cup (60ml) peanut oil

1 tablespoon finely grated lemon rind

2 cloves garlic, crushed

2 lebanese cucumbers (260g)

1 medium red capsicum (200g), sliced thinly

140g watercress

1 tablespoon water

1 Cut squid in half lengthways; score inside surface of each piece, diagonally, into 2cm-wide strips.

2 Combine cumin, dill, juice, sauces and oil in small jug; mix well.

3 Combine squid, rind and garlic in large bowl with half of the cumin mixture. Cover; refrigerate 1 hour. Cover remaining cumin mixture; refrigerate until required.

4 Drain squid; discard marinade.

5 Cook squid on heated oiled barbecue, uncovered, until browned all over and cooked through; cover to keep warm.

6 Halve cucumbers lengthways; cut into thin slices. Combine cucumber with capsicum and watercress in large bowl.

7 Stir the water into reserved cumin mixture. Pour over salad; toss gently to combine. Serve squid with salad.

serves 4

per serving 17.5g fat; 1606kJ

tip Squid can be substituted with baby octopus, if preferred.

tuna with char-grilled vegetables

PREPARATION TIME 10 MINUTES ■ COOKING TIME 35 MINUTES

3 medium potatoes (600g)

2 medium lemons (280g)

**2 pickled baby dill cucumbers,
  sliced thinly**

4 small tuna steaks (600g)

**2 teaspoons drained
  green peppercorns**

2 teaspoons drained tiny capers

1 Boil, steam or microwave potatoes until just tender; cut each potato into four slices. Cut each lemon into six slices.

2 Cook potato, lemon and cucumber, in batches, on heated oiled barbecue, uncovered, until browned both sides.

3 Cook tuna on heated oiled barbecue, uncovered, until browned both sides and cooked as desired.

4 Cook peppercorns and capers on heated oiled barbecue until hot.

5 Divide potato among plates; top with tuna, lemon and cucumber. Sprinkle with peppercorns and capers.

serves 4

per serving 8.8g fat; 1382kJ

asian-style fish

PREPARATION TIME 15 MINUTES ■ COOKING TIME 20 MINUTES

4 x 350g bream
6 green onions, sliced thinly
50g fresh ginger, sliced thinly
4 cloves garlic, sliced thinly
2 tablespoons soy sauce
2 tablespoons dry sherry
2 tablespoons brown sugar
⅓ cup (80ml) vegetable stock
500g choy sum, chopped coarsely
500g chinese broccoli, chopped coarsely

1 Score fish three times on each side.

2 Place fish on four large pieces of oiled foil.

3 Combine onion, ginger, garlic, sauce, sherry, sugar and stock in small bowl; divide mixture over fish. Wrap fish securely in foil.

4 Place fish on heated oiled barbecue; cook, covered, using indirect heat, following manufacturer's instructions, 20 minutes or until cooked through.

5 Meanwhile, boil, steam or microwave choy sum and broccoli, separately, until just wilted; drain.

6 Transfer fish and onion mixture to serving plates. Serve with vegetables.

serves 4

per serving 8.8g fat; 1382kJ
tip Fish can be assembled and wrapped in foil several hours ahead; prevent the sauce leaking out by using a double layer of foil. Refrigerate fish parcels until cooking time.

thai-style fish cutlets

PREPARATION TIME 15 MINUTES ■ COOKING TIME 20 MINUTES

4 blue-eye cutlets (1kg)

4 green onions, sliced thinly

4 kaffir lime leaves, shredded thinly

**80g fresh ginger, peeled,
    sliced thinly**

**¼ cup coarsely chopped
    fresh coriander**

2 tablespoons sweet chilli sauce

2 tablespoons lime juice

2 tablespoons brown sugar

2 teaspoons peanut oil

1 teaspoon fish sauce

1 Place cutlets on four large pieces of oiled foil; top each cutlet with equal amounts of onion, lime leaf, ginger and coriander. Drizzle with combined remaining ingredients; fold foil over the top, pinching it tightly to enclose cutlets.

2 Place foil parcels on heated oiled barbecue; cook, covered, using indirect heat, following manufacturer's instructions, 20 minutes or until cooked through. Serve with salad, if desired.

serves 4

per serving   7.8g fat; 1273kJ

blackened fish with burnt lemon butter

PREPARATION TIME 10 MINUTES ■ COOKING TIME 10 MINUTES

4 salmon steaks (720g)

20g butter, melted

**2 teaspoons cracked
   black pepper**

1½ teaspoons sweet paprika

1½ teaspoons dried thyme

1½ teaspoons mustard powder

1½ teaspoons ground cumin

BURNT LEMON BUTTER

60g butter, melted

1 tablespoon lemon juice

2 green onions, chopped finely

1 Brush both sides of fish with butter; sprinkle evenly with combined remaining ingredients.

2 Cook fish on heated oiled barbecue, uncovered, until browned both sides and cooked as desired.

3 Serve fish drizzled with burnt lemon butter; accompany with mashed potatoes and barbecued lemon halves, if desired.

burnt lemon butter Melt butter in small saucepan on barbecue hotplate until browned; stir in juice and onion.

serves 4

per serving 29.6g fat; 1728kJ

balmain bugs with oregano

PREPARATION TIME 20 MINUTES (plus marinating time) ■ COOKING TIME 15 MINUTES

8 medium uncooked balmain bugs (1kg)
2 tablespoons dry white wine
2 tablespoons lime juice
2 tablespoons olive oil
2 tablespoons coarsely chopped fresh oregano
2 cloves garlic, crushed

1 Cut balmain bugs in half lengthways; clean.

2 Combine wine, juice, oil, half of the oregano and garlic in large bowl; add balmain bugs. Cover; refrigerate 1 hour.

3 Cook balmain bugs on heated oiled barbecue, uncovered, until browned and cooked through. Serve sprinkled with remaining oregano.

serves 4

per serving 11g fat; 1206kJ

pesto fish kebabs

PREPARATION TIME 20 MINUTES (plus marinating time) ■ COOKING TIME 15 MINUTES

600g firm white fish fillets

1 tablespoon bottled pesto

**½ cup finely chopped fresh
flat-leaf parsley**

**½ small savoy cabbage (600g),
shredded finely**

⅓ cup (65g) drained baby capers

1 teaspoon finely grated lemon rind

½ cup finely chopped fresh mint

1 Cut fish into 2cm cubes; combine with pesto and 1 tablespoon of the parsley in medium bowl. Cover; refrigerate 1 hour.

2 Thread fish onto eight skewers.

3 Cook fish on heated oiled barbecue, uncovered, until browned and just cooked through. Cover to keep warm.

4 Cook cabbage on heated oiled barbecue plate, uncovered, until just tender. Stir in remaining parsley, capers, rind and mint.

5 Serve fish with cabbage mixture.

serves 4

per serving 5.5g fat; 870kJ

tip If using bamboo skewers, soak in water for at least 1 hour before using, to avoid scorching.

fish steaks with tomato and chilli butter

PREPARATION TIME 20 MINUTES (plus marinating and refrigeration time) ■ COOKING TIME 10 MINUTES

6 swordfish steaks (1.2kg)

1 teaspoon grated lime rind

¼ cup (60ml) lime juice

TOMATO AND CHILLI BUTTER

125g butter

**⅓ cup (50g) drained, finely chopped
    sun-dried tomatoes**

1 tablespoon lime juice

1 tablespoon sambal oelek

**1 tablespoon finely chopped
    fresh flat-leaf parsley**

1 Combine fish, rind and juice in large shallow dish. Cover; refrigerate 30 minutes.

2 Drain fish; discard marinade.

3 Cook fish on heated oiled barbecue, uncovered, until browned both sides and
    just cooked through.

4 Serve with tomato and chilli butter.

   tomato and chilli butter Beat butter in small bowl with electric mixer until
   light and fluffy; add tomato, juice, sambal oelek and parsley. Spoon mixture
   onto greaseproof paper or foil. Roll up firmly; shape into log. Refrigerate
   1 hour or until firm.

   serves 6

   per serving 22.3g fat; 1608kJ
   tip Tomato and chilli butter can be made a week ahead and refrigerated, covered.

chilli plum crabs

PREPARATION TIME 20 MINUTES (plus marinating time) ■ COOKING TIME 15 MINUTES

6 uncooked blue swimmer crabs

½ cup (125ml) plum sauce

½ cup (125ml) sweet chilli sauce

2 tablespoons oyster sauce

2 tablespoons peanut oil

1 tablespoon soy sauce

1 clove garlic, crushed

1 tablespoon grated fresh ginger

½ teaspoon sesame oil

1 Remove triangular flap from underside of each crab. Remove top shell and grey fibrous tissue; wash crabs. Crack nippers slightly; cut crabs in half.

2 Combine remaining ingredients in large bowl; add crab. Cover; refrigerate 3 hours or overnight.

3 Cook crab on heated oiled barbecue, uncovered, until cooked through.

serves 6

per serving 9.4g fat; 1489kJ

soy and chilli fish parcels

PREPARATION TIME 15 MINUTES ■ COOKING TIME 15 MINUTES

Kecap manis, also known as ketjap manis, is a sweet, thick soy sauce available from some supermarkets and Asian food stores.

4 flathead fillets (600g)

1½ cups (120g) bean sprouts

3 cloves garlic, crushed

4 green onions, sliced thinly

¼ teaspoon sesame oil

2 tablespoons kecap manis

2 fresh red thai chillies, seeded, chopped finely

2 teaspoons sweet sherry

1 Divide fish among four large pieces of oiled foil. Divide sprouts among fish; top with combined remaining ingredients. Seal foil to enclose fish.

2 Place fish on heated oiled barbecue. Cook, covered, using indirect heat, following manufacturer's instructions, 15 minutes or until cooked through.

serves 4

per serving   1.9g fat; 680kJ

nutty rice snapper

PREPARATION TIME 20 MINUTES ■ COOKING TIME 1 HOUR 10 MINUTES

You will need to cook about ¾ cup (150g) rice for this recipe.

2kg whole snapper

SEASONING

60g butter

1 medium brown onion (150g), chopped finely

2 cloves garlic, crushed

1 tablespoon ground coriander

1 tablespoon ground cumin

2 teaspoons mustard powder

2 teaspoons sweet paprika

2 teaspoons mild curry powder

2 cups cooked long grain rice

½ cup (75g) pistachios, toasted

2 tablespoons coarsely chopped fresh flat-leaf parsley

2 tablespoons coarsely chopped fresh coriander leaves

2 teaspoons finely grated lemon rind

1 Score fish three times on each side.

2 Fill cavity of fish with seasoning; wrap in lightly oiled foil.

3 Place fish on heated oiled barbecue; cook, covered, using indirect heat, following manufacturer's instructions, about 1 hour or until cooked through.

seasoning Melt butter in medium frying pan; cook onion and garlic until onion is soft. Add spices; cook, stirring, until fragrant. Combine onion mixture, rice, nuts, herbs and rind in large bowl.

serves 8

per serving 14.6g fat; 1687kJ

swordfish with olive paste

PREPARATION TIME 15 MINUTES ■ COOKING TIME 10 MINUTES

200g kalamata olives, seeded
¼ cup (50g) drained capers
⅓ cup finely chopped fresh dill
⅓ cup finely chopped fresh flat-leaf parsley
2 cloves garlic, crushed
2 tablespoons lemon juice
4 swordfish steaks (800g)

1 Blend or process olives, capers, dill, parsley, garlic and juice until mixture forms an almost smooth paste.

2 Cook fish on heated oiled barbecue, uncovered, until browned both sides and just cooked through. Spread olive paste over fish to serve.

serves 4

per serving 5g fat; 1067kJ

tip Olive paste can be made 3 days ahead and refrigerated, covered.

cajun seafood kebabs with avocado salsa

PREPARATION TIME 30 MINUTES ■ COOKING TIME 10 MINUTES

800g medium uncooked prawns

800g firm white fish fillets

2 tablespoons cajun seasoning

2 teaspoons ground cumin

2 tablespoons coarsely chopped fresh oregano

2 cloves garlic, crushed

¼ cup (60ml) olive oil

AVOCADO SALSA

1 large avocado (320g), chopped finely

3 medium tomatoes (570g), seeded, chopped finely

1 small red onion (100g), chopped finely

2 tablespoons finely chopped fresh coriander

2 tablespoons lemon juice

1 tablespoon olive oil

½ teaspoon sugar

1 Peel and devein prawns leaving tails intact. Cut fish into 3cm pieces.

2 Combine prawns and fish with remaining ingredients in medium bowl. Cover; refrigerate 1 hour.

3 Thread prawns and fish onto 12 skewers.

4 Cook seafood on heated oiled barbecue, uncovered, until browned and cooked through.

5 Serve with avocado salsa.

avocado salsa Combine ingredients in medium bowl.

serves 6

per serving 24.2g fat; 1681kJ
tip If using bamboo skewers, soak in water for at least 1 hour before using, to avoid scorching.

grilled lime and pepper ocean trout

PREPARATION TIME 10 MINUTES (plus marinating time) ■ COOKING TIME 10 MINUTES

2 teaspoons grated lime rind

½ teaspoon cracked black pepper

2 tablespoons olive oil

2 tablespoons finely chopped fresh chives

4 ocean trout cutlets (720g)

1 large red onion (300g)

2 limes

1 Combine rind, pepper, oil and chives in large bowl. Add fish; turn to coat in mixture. Cover; refrigerate 1 hour.

2 Meanwhile, cut onion and limes into wedges.

3 Cook fish, onion and lime on heated oiled barbecue, uncovered, until fish is browned both sides and just cooked through, and onion and lime are browned.

4 Serve fish with onion and lime.

serves 4

per serving 15.6g fat; 1268kJ

cumin fish cutlets with coriander chilli sauce

PREPARATION TIME 15 MINUTES ■ COOKING TIME 10 MINUTES

6 salmon cutlets (1.2kg)
2 teaspoons cumin seeds

CORIANDER CHILLI SAUCE
8 green onions, chopped coarsely
3 cloves garlic, crushed
3 fresh red thai chillies, seeded, chopped finely
1 tablespoon finely chopped coriander root
2 tablespoons brown sugar
2 tablespoons fish sauce
¼ cup (60ml) lime juice

1 Sprinkle one side of each cutlet with cumin seeds.

2 Cook fish on heated oiled barbecue, uncovered, until browned both sides and cooked as desired.

3 Serve fish with coriander chilli sauce; accompany with fried potatoes, if desired.

coriander chilli sauce Using the "pulse" button, blend or process onion, garlic, chilli, coriander root and sugar until chopped finely. Add sauce and juice; blend until combined.

serves 6

per serving 13.4g fat; 1225kJ

cutlets with artichokes

PREPARATION TIME 15 MINUTES ■ COOKING TIME 25 MINUTES

Any commercially made pesto based on basil is suitable.

⅔ cup (180g) basil pesto

1 cup firmly packed fresh basil leaves

2 x 400g cans artichoke hearts, drained, halved

1 large red onion (300g), sliced thinly

2 large mushrooms (300g), peeled, sliced thickly

2 baby eggplants (120g), sliced lengthways

4 blue-eye cutlets (1kg)

½ cup finely shredded fresh basil, extra

1 Blend or process pesto and basil until combined; reserve ¼ cup of the pesto mixture.

2 Combine artichoke, onion, mushroom, eggplant and half of the remaining pesto mixture in large bowl.

3 Cook vegetable mixture on heated oiled barbecue, uncovered, until browned and tender. Cover; keep warm.

4 Brush fish with reserved pesto mixture. Cook fish on heated oiled barbecue until browned and cooked through.

5 Combine remaining pesto mixture, extra basil and char-grilled vegetables in large bowl.

6 Serve vegetables topped with fish.

serves 4

per serving 21.6g fat; 1937kJ

spiced trout with cucumber and yogurt

PREPARATION TIME 10 MINUTES ■ COOKING TIME 10 MINUTES

4 small ocean trout fillets (1.2kg)

1 tablespoon olive oil

2 teaspoons ground cumin

1 teaspoon ground paprika

½ teaspoon ground chilli

1 lebanese cucumber (130g)

⅓ cup (95g) yogurt

**2 tablespoons finely chopped
fresh mint**

1 Brush fish with oil; sprinkle with combined cumin, paprika and chilli.

2 Cut cucumber into thin slices, then into fine strips; drain on absorbent paper.

3 Cook fish on heated oiled barbecue, uncovered, until browned both sides and just cooked through.

4 Serve fish topped with cucumber, yogurt and mint; accompany with baby spinach leaves and sliced tiny new potatoes, if desired.

serves 4

per serving 17g fat; 1693kJ

sweet chilli lime fish

PREPARATION TIME 10 MINUTES ■ COOKING TIME 10 MINUTES

½ cup (125ml) sweet chilli sauce
¼ cup coarsely chopped fresh coriander
2 tablespoons lime juice
1 teaspoon sesame oil
1.2kg flathead fillets

1 Combine sauce, coriander, juice and oil in large bowl; add fish.

2 Cook fish on heated oiled barbecue, uncovered, until browned both sides and just cooked through.

serves 6

per serving 3.4g fat; 926kJ

spinach and fetta damper

PREPARATION TIME 20 MINUTES
COOKING TIME 40 MINUTES

3½ cups (525g) self-raising flour
1 teaspoon salt
2 teaspoons cracked black pepper
1 tablespoon sugar
40g butter
200g fetta cheese, crumbled
200g baby spinach leaves, chopped finely
½ cup (125ml) buttermilk
1 cup (250ml) water, approximately

1 Combine flour, salt, pepper and sugar in large bowl; rub in butter.

2 Stir in cheese, spinach, buttermilk and enough of the water to make a soft, sticky dough.

3 Turn dough onto floured surface; knead until just smooth. Divide dough in half; place in greased disposable baking dish. Press each half into a 10cm round. Cut a cross in dough; about 1cm deep. Brush with a little extra buttermilk, then sift a little extra flour over dough.

4 Cook in covered barbecue, using indirect heat, following manufacturer's instructions, about 40 minutes or until cooked.

serves 6

per serving 14.8g fat; 1951kJ

olive tapenade and mozzarella turkish bread

PREPARATION TIME 10 MINUTES
COOKING TIME 10 MINUTES

⅔ cup (80g) seeded black olives
2 tablespoons finely chopped fresh flat-leaf parsley
2 teaspoons grated lemon rind
1 tablespoon lemon juice
1 clove garlic, crushed
2 tablespoons drained capers
40cm loaf turkish bread
250g mozzarella cheese, sliced thinly

1 Blend or process olives, parsley, rind, juice, garlic and capers until almost smooth.

2 Place bread on oven tray. Spread top with olive tapenade; top with cheese.

3 Cook in covered barbecue, using indirect heat, following manufacturer's instructions, about 10 minutes or until cheese melts and is browned lightly.

serves 4

per serving 16.2g fat; 1720kJ

pesto bread

PREPARATION TIME 10 MINUTES
COOKING TIME 5 MINUTES

We used bottled basil pesto and char-grilled vegetable pesto,
available from most supermarkets.

40cm loaf ciabatta
1/4 cup (60ml) olive oil
1/4 cup (65g) basil pesto
1/4 cup (65g) char-grilled vegetable pesto

1 Cut bread diagonally into 12 slices. Brush bread
  slices lightly with oil.

2 Cook bread on heated oiled barbecue, uncovered,
  until toasted lightly both sides.

3 Spread half of the slices with basil pesto; spread
  remaining slices with char-grilled vegetable pesto.

serves 6

per serving 19.3g fat; 1577kJ

bruschetta

PREPARATION TIME 15 MINUTES
COOKING TIME 5 MINUTES

2 large tomatoes (500g), chopped coarsely
1 small red onion (100g), chopped finely
1 clove garlic, crushed
2 tablespoons olive oil
1/2 teaspoon sugar
2 tablespoons shredded fresh basil
40cm loaf ciabatta
1/4 cup (60ml) olive oil, extra

1 Combine tomato, onion, garlic, oil, sugar and
  basil in medium bowl.

2 Cut bread into 1.5cm thick slices; drizzle with
  extra oil. Cook bread on heated oiled barbecue,
  uncovered, until toasted lightly both sides.

3 Serve tomato mixture on toasted bread.

serves 6

per serving 17.7g fat; 1554kJ

breads

poultry

Poultry and barbecues are made for each other – golden sticky wings, marinated breasts threaded on skewers, and flattened chicken halves in the incomparable Portuguese style. Other barbecued birds, such as quail and turkey, are just as delicious.

sweet chilli chicken drumsticks

PREPARATION TIME 10 MINUTES (plus marinating time) ■ COOKING TIME 20 MINUTES

12 chicken drumsticks (1.8kg)

²⁄₃ cup (160ml) sweet chilli sauce

2 cloves garlic, crushed

2 tablespoons fish sauce

2 tablespoons brown sugar

**1 tablespoon finely chopped
   fresh lemon grass**

1 Place chicken in large saucepan; cover with cold water. Bring to a boil; reduce heat. Simmer, covered, about 10 minutes or until chicken is just cooked through; drain.

2 Meanwhile, combine remaining ingredients in small bowl.

3 Place chicken in shallow dish with half of the chilli mixture. Cover; refrigerate 3 hours or overnight.

4 Cook undrained chicken on heated oiled barbecue, uncovered, until browned all over and cooked through, brushing with the remaining chilli mixture during cooking. Serve with char-grilled vegetables, if desired.

serves 4

per serving 40.1g fat; 2617kJ

tip Do not have the barbecue too hot as the sweet marinade will burn before the chicken is heated through.

chutney chicken breast with kashmiri pilaf

PREPARATION TIME 10 MINUTES ■ COOKING TIME 25 MINUTES

While many Indian dishes involve long, slow cooking, this recipe captures the essence of the cuisine in a quick and easy char-grill.

1 tablespoon vegetable oil

1 small brown onion (80g), chopped finely

1 clove garlic, crushed

1 teaspoon black mustard seeds

¼ teaspoon ground cardamom

½ teaspoon ground cumin

½ teaspoon garam masala

½ teaspoon ground turmeric

1½ cups (300g) white long-grain rice

3 cups (750ml) chicken stock

2 tablespoons coarsely chopped fresh coriander

⅓ cup (110g) mango chutney

2 tablespoons water

4 single chicken breast fillets (700g)

1 Heat oil in medium saucepan; cook onion, garlic and mustard seeds, stirring, until onion softens and seeds pop. Add remaining spices; cook, stirring, until fragrant.

2 Add rice; stir to coat in spices. Add stock; bring to a boil. Reduce heat; simmer, uncovered, until rice is just tender. Stir in coriander.

3 Meanwhile, combine chutney with the water in small saucepan; cook, stirring, until heated through and well combined.

4 Cook chicken, brushing all over with chutney mixture, on heated oiled barbecue, uncovered, until browned both sides and cooked through. Cut into thick slices. Serve chutney chicken with pilaf.

serves 4

per serving 15.6g fat; 2539kJ

tip Do not have the barbecue too hot as the mango chutney will burn before the chicken is cooked through.

tandoori drumsticks

PREPARATION TIME 10 MINUTES (plus marinating time) ■ COOKING TIME 20 MINUTES

12 chicken drumsticks (1.8kg)
½ cup (140g) yogurt
2 teaspoons ground cumin
2 teaspoons ground coriander
1 teaspoon sweet paprika
2 cloves garlic, crushed
few drops red food colouring
½ cup (160g) lime pickle
½ cup (160g) mango chutney

1 Score each chicken drumstick three times.

2 Combine yogurt, spices, garlic and food colouring in large bowl; add chicken. Cover; refrigerate 3 hours or overnight.

3 Cook undrained chicken on heated oiled barbecue, uncovered, until browned all over and cooked through.

4 Serve chicken with pickle and chutney.

serves 4

per serving 40.7g fat; 2855kJ

chicken satay

PREPARATION TIME 30 MINUTES (plus marinating time) ■ COOKING TIME 15 MINUTES

12 chicken thigh fillets (1.3kg)

2 tablespoons mild sweet chilli sauce

1 tablespoon peanut oil

1 clove garlic, crushed

2 tablespoons coarsely chopped fresh coriander

PEANUT SAUCE

1 cup (250ml) chicken stock

1/2 cup (130g) crunchy peanut butter

1/4 cup (60ml) mild sweet chilli sauce

1 tablespoon lemon juice

1 Cut each chicken fillet into four strips lengthways.

2 Combine sauce, oil, garlic and coriander in medium bowl; add chicken. Cover; refrigerate 3 hours or overnight.

3 Thread chicken onto 12 skewers.

4 Cook chicken on heated oil barbecue, uncovered, until browned and cooked through.

5 Serve chicken with peanut sauce, rice and bok choy, if desired.

peanut sauce Combine ingredients in medium saucepan on barbecue hotplate; simmer, stirring, about 3 minutes or until sauce thickens slightly.

serves 6

per serving 30.2g fat; 2011kJ

tips If using bamboo skewers, soak in water for at least 1 hour before using, to avoid scorching. Uncooked marinated skewers are suitable to freeze; the peanut sauce is suitable to microwave.

mustard rosemary chicken

PREPARATION TIME 10 MINUTES (plus marinating time) ■ COOKING TIME 15 MINUTES

2 tablespoons lemon juice

¼ cup (60ml) olive oil

2 cloves garlic, crushed

2 tablespoons coarsely chopped fresh rosemary

¼ cup (60g) seeded mustard

1kg chicken thigh fillets

½ cup (125ml) dry white wine

300ml cream

1 teaspoon cornflour

1 teaspoon water

1 tablespoon coarsely chopped fresh rosemary, extra

1 Combine juice, oil, garlic, rosemary and mustard in medium bowl; add chicken. Cover; refrigerate 3 hours or overnight.

2 Drain chicken; reserve marinade.

3 Cook chicken on heated oiled barbecue, uncovered, until browned both sides and cooked through.

4 Place reserved marinade and wine in small saucepan on barbecue hotplate; bring to a boil. Reduce heat; simmer until reduced by half. Stir in cream, then blended cornflour and water; bring to a boil, stirring, until mixture thickens slightly.

5 Serve chicken with sauce and steamed baby carrots, if desired; sprinkle with extra rosemary.

serves 4

per serving 64.9g fat; 3390kJ

indian spatchcock with
green chilli and coriander

PREPARATION TIME 25 MINUTES (plus marinating time) ■ COOKING TIME 45 MINUTES

4 x 500g spatchcocks
1 cup firmly packed fresh coriander leaves
6 green thai chillies, seeded, chopped finely
8 cloves garlic, chopped coarsely
2 tablespoons grated fresh ginger
2 tablespoons garam masala
½ cup (125ml) lemon juice

1 Rinse spatchcocks under cold running water; pat dry with absorbent paper. Using kitchen scissors, cut along each side of backbone; discard backbone. Place spatchcocks, skin-side up, on board. Using heel of hand, press down on breastbone to flatten spatchcocks.

2 Blend or process remaining ingredients until pureed.

3 Combine spatchcock and pureed mixture in large bowl. Cover; refrigerate 3 hours or overnight.

4 Place undrained spatchcock in single layer on oiled wire rack in disposable baking dish. Cook spatchcock in covered barbecue, using indirect heat, following manufacturer's instructions, about 45 minutes or until browned and cooked through.

serves 4

per serving 47.3g fat; 2816kJ

sweet-and-spicy quail

PREPARATION TIME 30 MINUTES (plus marinating time) ■ COOKING TIME 10 MINUTES

24 quails (4.8kg)

2 cups (540g) mango chutney

2 tablespoons cumin seeds

1 tablespoon sweet paprika

**1 tablespoon coarsely grated
    lemon rind**

1 cup (250ml) lemon juice

1 teaspoon cracked black pepper

4 cloves garlic, crushed

**1/2 cup coarsely chopped
    fresh coriander**

1 Remove and discard neck from quails. Cut along both sides of each backbone; discard backbones. Halve each quail along breastbone.

2 Combine chutney, cumin, paprika, rind, juice, pepper and garlic in large bowl; reserve 1/2 cup (125ml) of marinade.

3 Stir 1 tablespoon of the coriander into reserved marinade. Cover; refrigerate until required. Stir remaining coriander into marinade in bowl; add quail. Cover; refrigerate 3 hours or overnight.

4 Drain quail; discard marinade.

5 Cook quail on heated oiled barbecue, uncovered, until browned both sides and cooked through.

6 Serve with reserved marinade.

serves 8

per serving 38.3g fat; 3044kJ

tip This marinade is also suitable for chicken pieces or butterflied spatchcock.

thyme chicken with grilled citrus

PREPARATION TIME 15 MINUTES (plus marinating time) ■ COOKING TIME 15 MINUTES

2 tablespoons olive oil

2 teaspoons dijon mustard

2 tablespoons fresh thyme leaves

4 single chicken breast fillets (700g)

2 medium lemons (280g)

2 limes

¼ cup (60g) dijon mustard, extra

1 Combine oil, mustard and half of the thyme in medium bowl; add chicken. Cover; refrigerate 3 hours or overnight.

2 Drain chicken; reserve marinade.

3 Cook chicken on heated oiled barbecue, uncovered, until browned both sides and cooked through, brushing occasionally with reserved marinade during cooking.

4 Meanwhile, cut each lemon into six wedges and each lime into four wedges; cook on heated oiled barbecue until browned all over.

5 Combine extra mustard and remaining thyme in small bowl. Serve chicken with citrus wedges and mustard mixture.

serves 4

per serving 19.4g fat; 1470kJ

turkey with lime and mustard

PREPARATION TIME 10 MINUTES (plus marinating time) ■ COOKING TIME 5 MINUTES

Turkey breast escalopes are very thin slices of turkey breast fillet.

8 turkey breast escalopes (550g)
2 tablespoons olive oil
2 teaspoons cracked black pepper
1 tablespoon dijon mustard
1 teaspoon grated lime rind
2 tablespoons lime juice
2 limes, sliced thinly

1 Place turkey in large shallow dish; pour over combined oil, pepper, mustard, rind and juice. Cover; refrigerate 3 hours or overnight.

2 Drain turkey; discard marinade.

3 Cook turkey and lime on heated oiled barbecue, uncovered, until turkey is browned both sides and cooked through.

4 Serve turkey with barbecued lime and baby spinach leaves, if desired.

serves 4

per serving 13.8g fat; 1064kJ

herbed chicken kebabs with roasted pecans

PREPARATION TIME 15 MINUTES (plus marinating time) ■ COOKING TIME 15 MINUTES

**1kg chicken breast fillets,
  sliced thinly**

½ cup finely chopped fresh chives

⅓ cup finely chopped fresh oregano

**¼ cup finely chopped
  fresh marjoram**

4 cloves garlic, crushed

**1 tablespoon lemon
  pepper seasoning**

2 tablespoons chicken stock

**¼ cup (30g) chopped
  pecans, roasted**

1 Thread chicken onto 12 skewers.

2 Combine chives, oregano, marjoram, garlic, seasoning and stock in shallow dish; add chicken. Cover; refrigerate 3 hours or overnight.

3 Cook chicken on heated oiled barbecue, uncovered, until browned all over and cooked through.

4 Serve with pecans.

serves 6

per serving 12.9g fat; 1118kJ

tip If using bamboo skewers, soak in water for at least 1 hour before using, to avoid scorching.

sesame chicken cutlets

PREPARATION TIME 10 MINUTES (plus marinating time) ■ COOKING TIME 15 MINUTES

2 cloves garlic, crushed

1 tablespoon grated fresh ginger

¼ cup (60ml) soy sauce

¼ cup (60ml) hoisin sauce

2 teaspoons sesame oil

8 chicken thigh cutlets (1.3kg)

2 tablespoons sesame seeds, toasted

1 Combine garlic, ginger, sauces and oil in large bowl; add chicken. Cover; refrigerate 3 hours or overnight.

2 Drain chicken; reserve marinade.

3 Cook chicken on heated oiled barbecue, uncovered, until browned both sides and cooked through, brushing occasionally with reserved marinade during cooking.

4 Serve sprinkled with sesame seeds.

serves 4

per serving 35.2g fat; 2037kJ

portuguese chicken

PREPARATION TIME 15 MINUTES (plus marinating time) ■ COOKING TIME 1 HOUR 15 MINUTES

1.6kg whole chicken
½ cup (125ml) lemon juice
2 tablespoons olive oil
4 fresh red thai chillies, seeded, chopped finely
1 tablespoon brown sugar
1 tablespoon sweet paprika
1 clove garlic, crushed
2 teaspoons dried oregano
2 teaspoons salt

1 Rinse chicken under cold running water; pat dry with absorbent paper. Using kitchen scissors, cut along both sides of backbone; discard backbone. Place chicken, skin-side up, on board; using heel of hand, press down on breastbone to flatten chicken. Insert metal skewer through thigh and opposite wing of chicken to keep chicken flat. Repeat with other thigh and wing.

2 Place chicken in large shallow dish; pour over combined remaining ingredients. Cover; refrigerate 3 hours or overnight.

3 Drain chicken; reserve marinade.

4 Place chicken on oiled wire rack over disposable baking dish; pour over reserved marinade. Cook in covered barbecue, using indirect heat, following manufacturer's instructions, about 1¼ hours or until browned and cooked through, brushing occasionally with pan juices during cooking.

5 Serve with a crispy garden salad and crusty bread, if desired.

serves 4

per serving 41.6g fat; 2288kJ

bombay-spiced chicken skewers

PREPARATION TIME 30 MINUTES (plus marinating time) ■ COOKING TIME 15 MINUTES (plus cooling time)

⅓ cup (80ml) peanut oil

4 cloves garlic, crushed

2 tablespoons sweet paprika

1 tablespoon ground cumin

1 tablespoon ground turmeric

1 tablespoon ground coriander

2kg chicken breast fillets

RAITA

2 lebanese cucumbers (260g), seeded, chopped finely

¾ cup (210g) yogurt

1 tablespoon lemon juice

2 cloves garlic, crushed

¼ cup finely chopped fresh mint

1 Heat oil in medium frying pan; cook garlic and spices, stirring, until fragrant; cool.

2 Cut chicken into 3cm pieces. Thread onto 24 skewers; place chicken in large shallow dish. Pour over spiced oil mixture; turn chicken to coat well. Cover; refrigerate 3 hours or overnight.

3 Drain chicken; discard marinade.

4 Cook chicken on heated oiled barbecue, uncovered, until browned and cooked through. Serve chicken with raita.

raita Combine ingredients in small bowl.

serves 8

per serving 29.5 fat; 2096kJ

tip If using bamboo skewers, soak in water for at least 1 hour before using, to avoid scorching.

mediterranean chicken

PREPARATION TIME 30 MINUTES ■ COOKING TIME 1 HOUR 15 MINUTES

2 fresh red thai chillies, seeded, chopped finely

4 cloves garlic, crushed

1 tablespoon ground cumin

1 tablespoon ground coriander

1 tablespoon finely grated lemon rind

1 tablespoon lemon juice

1 tablespoon olive oil

1.6kg whole chicken

1 lemon

1 Combine chilli, garlic, spices, rind, juice and oil in small bowl.

2 Rinse chicken under cold running water; pat dry with absorbent paper. Using kitchen scissors, cut along both sides of backbone; discard backbone. Place chicken, skin-side up, on board; using heel of hand, press down on breastbone to flatten chicken. Insert metal skewer through thigh and opposite wing to keep chicken flat. Repeat with other thigh and wing.

3 Using spatula or back of metal spoon, spread chilli mixture all over chicken. Cut lemon into eight wedges; place lemon and chicken on oiled wire rack over disposable baking dish. Cook in covered barbecue, using indirect heat, following manufacturer's instructions, about 1 1/4 hours or until browned and cooked through.

4 Serve chicken with salad, lebanese bread and either hummus or baba ghanoush, if desired.

serves 4

per serving 37.3g fat; 2110kJ

chicken on lemon grass skewers

PREPARATION TIME 25 MINUTES (plus marinating time) ■ COOKING TIME 15 MINUTES

700g chicken breast fillets
8 lemon grass sticks
¼ cup (60ml) peanut oil
2 cloves garlic, crushed
1 tablespoon grated fresh ginger
2 tablespoons coarsely chopped fresh mint
2 tablespoons coarsely chopped fresh basil

1 Cut chicken into 3cm pieces. Using a thick bamboo skewer, pierce centre of chicken pieces; thread chicken onto lemon grass sticks.

2 Place chicken in shallow dish; pour over combined remaining ingredients. Cover; refrigerate 3 hours or overnight.

3 Drain chicken; discard marinade.

4 Cook chicken on heated oiled barbecue, uncovered, until browned and cooked through.

serves 4

per serving 23.4g fat; 1511kJ

lemon rosemary chicken with couscous seasoning

PREPARATION TIME 25 MINUTES (plus standing time) ■ COOKING TIME 2 HOURS

½ cup (125ml) boiling water

½ cup (100g) couscous

¼ cup (35g) dried currants

1 small red onion (100g),
    chopped finely

2 teaspoons finely grated lemon rind

1 tablespoon lemon juice

2 tablespoons shelled pistachios,
    toasted, chopped

1.6kg chicken

LEMON AND ROSEMARY GLAZE

20g butter

2 cloves garlic, crushed

¼ cup (50g) firmly packed
    brown sugar

½ cup (125ml) lemon juice

2 tablespoons dry white wine

2 teaspoons finely chopped
    fresh rosemary

1 Combine the water and couscous in medium heatproof bowl; stand, covered, 5 minutes or until water is absorbed. Fluff couscous with fork; stir in currants, onion, rind, juice and nuts.

2 Rinse chicken under cold running water; pat dry, inside and out, with absorbent paper. Fill chicken cavity with couscous seasoning; secure opening with toothpicks or small skewer.

3 Tuck wing tips under body; tie legs together with kitchen string.

4 Place chicken in oiled disposable baking dish; pour lemon and rosemary glaze over chicken.

5 Cook chicken in covered barbecue, using indirect heat, following manufacturer's instructions, about 1½ hours or until tender, brushing occasionally with pan juices during cooking.

6 Stand 10 minutes before carving. Serve chicken with pan juices.

lemon and rosemary glaze Melt butter in small saucepan; cook garlic, stirring, until fragrant. Add sugar, juice and wine; cook, stirring, without boiling, until sugar dissolves. Simmer, uncovered, about 15 minutes, or until thick and syrupy; stir in rosemary.

serves 4

per serving 39.8g fat; 2971kJ

marjoram and orange turkey

PREPARATION TIME 25 MINUTES ■ COOKING TIME 2 HOURS 30 MINUTES

You will need three small oranges for this recipe.

4kg turkey

2 small oranges (360g), quartered

6 fresh bay leaves

2 sprigs fresh marjoram

ORANGE BUTTER

¼ cup (60ml) dry white wine

**2 teaspoons finely grated
   orange rind**

100g butter, chopped

1 clove garlic, crushed

2 tablespoons brown sugar

2 tablespoons orange juice

1 Discard turkey neck and giblets. Rinse turkey under cold running water; pat dry inside and out with absorbent paper.

2 Tuck wings under body; place orange, bay leaves and marjoram loosely inside body cavity. Tuck trimmed neck flap under body, securing with toothpicks; tie legs together with kitchen string.

3 Place turkey on oiled wire rack over disposable baking dish; brush with orange butter.

4 Cook in covered barbecue, using indirect heat, following manufacturer's instructions, about 2½ hours or until browned all over and cooked through, brushing occasionally with orange butter during cooking. Cover wings with foil if turkey is over-browning.

orange butter Combine ingredients in small saucepan; cook, stirring, until combined and heated through.

serves 8

per serving 42g fat; 2606kJ

middle eastern spicy roasted spatchcocks

PREPARATION TIME 45 MINUTES (plus marinating time)
COOKING TIME 30 MINUTES

4 x 500g spatchcocks
2 teaspoons sweet paprika
2 cloves garlic, crushed
1 teaspoon cumin seeds
2 teaspoons yellow mustard seeds
1 tablespoon coarsely chopped fresh coriander
2 green onions, chopped coarsely
⅓ cup (110g) mango chutney
2 tablespoons olive oil

VINAIGRETTE
2 tablespoons olive oil
1 tablespoon lemon juice
½ teaspoon coarsely chopped fresh rosemary
¼ teaspoon sugar

1 Rinse spatchcocks under cold running water; pat dry with absorbent paper. Using kitchen scissors, cut along each side of backbone; discard backbone. Place spatchcocks, skin-side down, on board. Scrape meat away from rib cage; remove rib cage. Cut through thigh and wing joints without cutting skin.

2 Scrape meat from breastbones; remove breastbones. Cut spatchcocks in half.

3 Combine paprika, garlic, seeds, coriander, onion, chutney and oil in large bowl; add spatchcock. Cover; refrigerate 3 hours or overnight.

4 Drain spatchcocks; reserve marinade.

5 Place spatchcocks in single layer on oiled wire rack over disposable baking dish. Cook spatchcock in covered barbecue, using indirect heat, following manufacturer's instructions, about 30 minutes or until browned and cooked through, brushing occasionally with reserved marinade during cooking.

6 Serve spatchcocks with watercress sprigs, if desired. Drizzle with vinaigrette.

vinaigrette Combine ingredients in screw-top jar; shake well.

serves 4

per serving 58.8g fat; 3237kJ

chicken with lentil salsa

PREPARATION TIME 10 MINUTES ■ COOKING TIME 15 MINUTES

The spices of North Africa give the chicken a flavour-packed jolt in this dish. And, as it can be served hot or cold, this recipe is a good one to prepare-ahead.

2 teaspoons ground cumin

2 teaspoons ground coriander

1 teaspoon ground turmeric

12 chicken tenderloins (900g)

2 limes, cut into wedges

LENTIL SALSA

1½ cups (300g) red lentils

1 clove garlic, crushed

1 fresh red thai chilli, seeded, chopped finely

1 lebanese cucumber (130g), seeded, chopped finely

1 medium red capsicum (200g), chopped finely

¼ cup (60ml) lemon juice

2 tablespoons peanut oil

2 tablespoons coarsely chopped fresh coriander

1 Combine spices in medium bowl with chicken; toss to coat chicken with spices.

2 Cook chicken on heated oiled barbecue, uncovered, until browned both sides and cooked through.

3 Cook lime on heated oiled barbecue, until browned all over. Serve chicken with lentil salsa, lime wedges and lavash bread, if desired.

lentil salsa Cook lentils in large saucepan of boiling water, uncovered, until just tender; drain. Rinse under cold running water; drain. Place lentils in large bowl with remaining ingredients.

serves 4

per serving 14.4g fat; 2206kJ

lamb

Few foods are as mouth-watering as a lamb chop on the barbie.
But don't stop there – think of cutlets, kebabs and even roasts.
If you have a covered barbecue, don't miss the slow-cooked
greek lamb with lemon and potatoes (page 114).

chilli and honey lamb

PREPARATION TIME 10 MINUTES (plus marinating time) ■ COOKING TIME 15 MINUTES

2 cloves garlic, crushed
1 tablespoon seeded mustard
1 teaspoon grated lemon rind
2 tablespoons lemon juice
2 tablespoons honey
2 teaspoons curry powder
1 teaspoon sambal oelek
1 teaspoon ground turmeric
8 lamb cutlets (600g)

1 Combine garlic, mustard, rind, juice, honey, curry powder, sambal oelek and turmeric in medium bowl.

2 Rub mixture onto lamb; place in large bowl. Cover; refrigerate 3 hours or overnight.

3 Cook lamb on heated oiled barbecue, uncovered, until browned and cooked as desired.

4 Serve with char-grilled asparagus, red capsicum and lemon, if desired.

serves 4

per serving 7.3g fat; 781kJ

gremolata-crumbed roast leg of lamb

PREPARATION TIME 15 MINUTES (plus marinating time) ■ COOKING TIME 1 HOUR 40 MINUTES

1.7kg leg of lamb

¼ cup (60ml) lemon juice

4 cloves garlic, crushed

5 large potatoes (1.5kg)

1 medium brown onion (150g), chopped finely

2 trimmed sticks celery (150g), chopped finely

2 tablespoons plain flour

½ cup (125ml) dry red wine

2 cups (500ml) beef stock

2 sprigs fresh rosemary

1 tablespoon finely chopped fresh flat-leaf parsley

GREMOLATA

½ cup finely chopped fresh flat-leaf parsley

1 tablespoon finely grated lemon rind

2 cloves garlic, crushed

½ cup (35g) stale breadcrumbs

1 tablespoon olive oil

1 Combine lamb with juice and half of the garlic in large bowl. Cover; refrigerate 3 hours or overnight.

2 Cut each potato into eight wedges.

3 Place undrained lamb and potato in disposable baking dish. Cook lamb in covered barbecue, using indirect heat, following manufacturer's instructions, 1 hour.

4 Press gremolata onto lamb; cook in covered barbecue further 30 minutes or until lamb is cooked as desired.

5 Remove lamb and potato from baking dish. Cover; keep warm. Cook onion, celery and remaining garlic in baking dish in covered barbecue, stirring, until vegetables are soft. Stir in flour; cook, stirring, about 1 minute or until bubbling. Gradually stir in wine and stock. Add rosemary; cook, stirring, until gravy thickens. Strain gravy into medium jug.

6 Serve lamb and potato wedges with gravy; sprinkle with parsley.

gremolata Combine ingredients in small bowl.

serves 6

per serving 16.4g fat; 2200kJ

lamb souvlakia

PREPARATION TIME 40 MINUTES (plus marinating time) ■ COOKING TIME 15 MINUTES

1.5kg boned lamb shoulder
1/4 cup (60ml) olive oil
2 teaspoons finely grated lemon rind
1/2 cup (125ml) lemon juice
2 cloves garlic, crushed
2 tablespoons finely chopped fresh oregano
1 1/2 cups (420g) yogurt
2 lebanese cucumbers (260g), seeded, chopped finely
2 cloves garlic, crushed, extra
8 large pitta
4 medium tomatoes (760g), sliced thinly

1 Trim fat from lamb; cut lamb into 3cm pieces. Combine oil, rind, juice, garlic and oregano in large bowl; add lamb. Cover; refrigerate 3 hours or overnight.

2 Combine yogurt, cucumber and extra garlic in small bowl. Cover; refrigerate 3 hours or overnight.

3 Thread lamb onto 16 skewers.

4 Cook lamb on heated oiled barbecue, uncovered, until browned and cooked as desired.

5 Serve souvlakia with cucumber yogurt, pitta and tomato.

serves 8

per serving 21.5g fat; 2678kJ
tip If using bamboo skewers, soak in water for at least 1 hour before using, to avoid scorching.

lamb in fruity chutney marinade

PREPARATION TIME 5 MINUTES (plus marinating time) ■ COOKING TIME 15 MINUTES

½ **cup (160g) fruit chutney**

2 tablespoons olive oil

2 teaspoons french mustard

½ **teaspoon cracked black pepper**

4 lamb forequarter chops (760g)

1 Combine chutney, oil, mustard and pepper in large bowl; add lamb. Cover; refrigerate 3 hours or overnight.

2 Cook lamb on heated oiled barbecue, uncovered, until browned and cooked as desired.

3 Serve with saffron rice and pappadums, if desired.

serves 4

per serving   17.9g fat; 1470kJ

tandoori lamb naan

PREPARATION TIME 15 MINUTES (plus marinating time) ■ COOKING TIME 10 MINUTES

¾ cup (210g) yogurt

1 tablespoon tandoori paste

4 lamb fillets (320g)

2 tablespoons coarsely chopped
   fresh mint

1 tablespoon lime juice

4 naan

100g curly endive

1 lebanese cucumber (130g),
   seeded, sliced thinly

1 Combine a third of the yogurt and paste in medium bowl; add lamb. Cover; refrigerate 3 hours or overnight.

2 Blend or process remaining yogurt, mint and juice until smooth. Cover; refrigerate until required.

3 Cook lamb on heated oiled barbecue, uncovered, until browned and cooked as desired. Cover; stand 5 minutes before slicing.

4 Meanwhile, heat naan according to directions on packet.

5 Place lamb, endive, cucumber and yogurt mixture in centre of naan; roll to enclose filling.

serves 4

per serving   15.5g fat; 1722kJ

lamb kofta with hummus and tabbouleh

PREPARATION TIME 1 HOUR (plus standing time) ■ COOKING TIME 15 MINUTES

½ cup (80g) burghul

1kg minced lamb

1 small brown onion (80g), chopped finely

1 teaspoon allspice

1 clove garlic, crushed

1 cup (75g) stale breadcrumbs

1 egg, beaten lightly

¾ cup (210g) yogurt

¼ cup finely chopped fresh mint

HUMMUS

2 x 300g cans chickpeas, rinsed, drained

1 teaspoon salt

1 clove garlic, quartered

⅓ cup (80ml) tahini

¼ cup (60ml) lemon juice

⅓ cup (80ml) water

TABBOULEH

¼ cup (40g) burghul

2 medium tomatoes (380g), seeded, chopped finely

4 cups coarsely chopped fresh flat-leaf parsley

1 small red onion (100g), chopped finely

2 tablespoons lemon juice

2 tablespoons olive oil

1 Cover burghul with cold water in small bowl; stand 20 minutes or until burghul softens. Drain burghul, squeezing with hands to remove as much water as possible.

2 Using hands, combine burghul with lamb, onion, allspice, garlic, breadcrumbs and egg in large bowl. Divide mixture into 12 balls; mould balls around 12 skewers to form sausage shape.

3 Cook kofta on heated oiled barbecue, uncovered, until browned and cooked through.

4 Serve kofta with hummus, tabbouleh and combined yogurt and mint.

hummus Blend or process ingredients until almost smooth.

tabbouleh Cover burghul with cold water in small bowl; stand 10 minutes or until burghul softens. Drain burghul, squeezing with hands to remove as much water as possible. Combine burghul in large bowl with remaining ingredients.

serves 6

per serving 35g fat; 2731kJ

tips If using bamboo skewers, soak in water for at least 1 hour before using, to avoid scorching. Lamb can be replaced with minced beef or chicken, if preferred.

lemon pepper cutlets with green pea puree

PREPARATION TIME 10 MINUTES ■ COOKING TIME 15 MINUTES

40g butter, chopped

1 medium brown onion (150g), chopped finely

⅓ cup (80ml) dry white wine

4 cups (500g) frozen green peas

1 teaspoon salt

12 lamb cutlets (900g), trimmed

300g marinated red capsicums, drained

1 tablespoon lemon pepper seasoning

1 Melt butter in medium saucepan; cook onion until soft.

2 Stir in wine, peas and salt; simmer, covered, 10 minutes. Blend or process mixture until smooth.

3 Meanwhile, cook lamb on heated oiled barbecue, uncovered, until browned and cooked as desired.

4 Cook capsicum on heated oiled barbecue until browned both sides.

5 Sprinkle lamb with seasoning; serve with pea puree and thickly sliced, char-grilled capsicum.

serves 4

per serving 30.7g fat; 2299kJ

sesame lamb

PREPARATION TIME 15 MINUTES (plus marinating and standing time) ■ COOKING TIME 15 MINUTES

1kg lamb eye of loin
2 cloves garlic, crushed
½ cup (175g) honey
2 teaspoons sesame oil
500g asparagus, trimmed
1 tablespoon sesame seeds, toasted

1 Combine lamb, garlic, honey and oil in large bowl. Cover; refrigerate 3 hours or overnight.

2 Drain lamb; discard marinade. Cook lamb on heated oiled barbecue until browned all over and cooked as desired. Stand 5 minutes; slice thinly.

3 Meanwhile, cook asparagus on heated oiled barbecue until tender.

4 Serve lamb with asparagus; sprinkle with seeds.

serves 4

per serving 13g fat; 1997kJ

greek lamb with lemon and potatoes

PREPARATION TIME 20 MINUTES (plus standing time)
COOKING TIME 4 HOURS

This recipe produces well-cooked but very moist, tender meat
which literally falls off the bone. This may make it difficult to carve,
in which case simply cut into chunks, or fork apart.

2kg leg of lamb
3 cloves garlic, quartered
6 sprigs fresh oregano, halved
1 large lemon (180g)
1kg old potatoes, peeled, quartered lengthways
1 teaspoon finely chopped fresh thyme

1 Make 12 small cuts in lamb with a sharp knife. Press
garlic and oregano into cuts.

2 Remove rind from lemon; cut rind into long thin strips
(or remove rind with a zester). Squeeze juice from
lemon – you will need 1/3 cup of juice.

3 Place lamb, upside down, in heavy-based baking
dish; pour juice over lamb. Cover dish lightly with
foil; cook in covered barbecue, using indirect heat,
following manufacturer's instructions, 2 hours. Turn
lamb over; brush all over with pan juices.

4 Add potato to dish; sprinkle with thyme and lemon
rind. Bake, covered, further 1 hour 45 minutes.

5 Remove foil; cook, uncovered, 15 minutes or until
browned. Stand lamb, loosely covered, 10 minutes
before serving.

serves 8

per serving 11.3g fat; 1408kJ

lamb with plum glaze

PREPARATION TIME 5 MINUTES (plus marinating time) ■ COOKING TIME 15 MINUTES

¾ cup (180ml) plum sauce
1 tablespoon soy sauce
2 cloves garlic, crushed
1 tablespoon dry sherry
8 lamb loin chops (800g)

1 Combine sauces, garlic and sherry in large bowl; add lamb. Cover; refrigerate 3 hours or overnight.

2 Cook lamb on heated oiled barbecue, uncovered, until browned and cooked as desired.

3 Serve with fried rice, if desired.

serves 4

per serving   13.5g fat; 1515kJ

lamb chermoulla with chickpea salad

PREPARATION TIME 20 MINUTES (plus marinating time) ■ COOKING TIME 15 MINUTES (plus standing time)

Chermoulla is a Moroccan mixture of fresh and ground spices including coriander, cumin and paprika. It can be used as a marinade for chicken, meat and fish.

2 teaspoons cracked black pepper

2 teaspoons ground cumin

2 teaspoons ground coriander

1 teaspoon hot paprika

2 tablespoons coarsely chopped fresh flat-leaf parsley

2 tablespoons coarsely chopped fresh coriander

2 tablespoons coarsely chopped fresh mint

1 tablespoon coarsely grated lemon rind

¼ cup (60ml) water

1 medium red onion (170g), chopped finely

8 lamb fillets (640g)

300g green beans, trimmed

400g can brown lentils, rinsed, drained

300g can chickpeas, rinsed, drained

⅓ cup coarsely chopped fresh flat-leaf parsley, extra

2 cloves garlic, crushed

2 tablespoons lemon juice

1 Blend or process pepper, spices, herbs, rind, the water and half of the onion until mixture forms a paste.

2 Coat lamb with chermoulla paste in large bowl. Cover; refrigerate 3 hours or overnight.

3 Cut beans into 3cm lengths; boil, steam or microwave beans until just tender. Refresh under cold water; drain.

4 Cook undrained lamb on heated oiled barbecue, uncovered, until browned and cooked as desired. Cover; stand 5 minutes before slicing thickly.

5 Combine beans, lentils, chickpeas, extra parsley, garlic and juice with remaining onion in large bowl; toss gently to combine.

6 Serve chickpea salad with lamb.

serves 4

per serving 7.7g fat; 1355kJ

pepper lamb steaks
with tomato jam

PREPARATION TIME 20 MINUTES (plus marinating time)
COOKING TIME 35 MINUTES

2 cloves garlic, crushed

2 tablespoons cracked black pepper

2 teaspoons finely chopped fresh thyme

2 teaspoons finely grated lemon rind

1 tablespoon plain flour

8 lamb steaks (1.6kg)

1 tablespoon olive oil

TOMATO JAM

3 medium tomatoes (570g), peeled, chopped coarsely

1 small white onion (80g), chopped finely

1 clove garlic, sliced thinly

1 cup (200g) firmly packed brown sugar

2 tablespoons malt vinegar

2 tablespoons lemon juice

1 Combine garlic, pepper, thyme, rind and flour in small bowl. Brush lamb with oil; press pepper mixture onto lamb. Cover; refrigerate 3 hours or overnight.

2 Cook lamb on heated oiled barbecue, uncovered, until browned and cooked as desired.

3 Serve lamb with tomato jam.

   tomato jam Combine tomato, onion and garlic in medium saucepan; bring to a boil. Boil, uncovered, about 3 minutes or until tomatoes are pulpy. Stir in sugar, vinegar and juice; boil, uncovered, about 15 minutes or until mixture becomes thick. Cool jam before serving.

serves 4

per serving 19.3g fat; 3070kJ
tip Jam can be made up to a week ahead and refrigerated, covered.

roast leg of lamb with garlic and rosemary

PREPARATION TIME 10 MINUTES ■ COOKING TIME 1 HOUR 30 MINUTES

2kg leg of lamb, trimmed

2 sprigs fresh rosemary, chopped coarsely

8 cloves garlic, sliced thinly

20g butter, softened

1 teaspoon cracked black pepper

1 Pierce lamb all over with sharp knife; place in large baking dish. Press rosemary and garlic firmly into cuts; rub combined butter and pepper over lamb.

2 Cook lamb in covered barbecue, using indirect heat, following manufacturer's instructions, about 1½ hours or until cooked as desired.

serves 6

per serving 17.7g fat; 1586kJ

kebabs with mint and pistachio pesto

PREPARATION TIME 20 MINUTES ■ COOKING TIME 15 MINUTES

1kg diced lamb

MINT AND PISTACHIO PESTO
**1 cup firmly packed fresh
    mint leaves**
⅓ cup (50g) pistachios, toasted
**⅓ cup (25g) coarsely grated
    parmesan cheese**
2 cloves garlic, crushed
1 tablespoon lemon juice
¼ cup (60ml) olive oil
2 tablespoons water, approximately

1 Thread lamb onto 12 skewers.

2 Cook lamb on heated oiled barbecue, uncovered, until browned and cooked as desired.

3 Serve lamb, with mint and pistachio pesto.

mint and pistachio pesto Blend or process mint, nuts, cheese, garlic and juice until well combined. With motor operating, gradually pour in oil and just enough of the water to give the desired consistency.

serves 6

per serving 26.1g fat; 1650kJ
tip If using bamboo skewers, soak in water for at least 1 hour before using, to avoid scorching.

garlic and rosemary smoked lamb

PREPARATION TIME 10 MINUTES (plus marinating and soaking time) ■ COOKING TIME 45 MINUTES

You will need 250g smoking chips for this recipe.

1kg boned rolled lamb loin
4 cloves garlic, halved
8 fresh rosemary sprigs
1 teaspoon dried chilli flakes
1 tablespoon olive oil

1 Place lamb in large shallow baking dish. Pierce lamb in eight places with sharp knife; push garlic and rosemary into cuts. Sprinkle lamb with chilli; rub with oil. Cover; refrigerate 3 hours or overnight.

2 Soak smoking chips in large bowl of water 2 hours.

3 Cook lamb on heated oiled barbecue, uncovered, until browned all over. Place drained chips in smoke box on barbecue next to lamb.

4 Cook lamb in covered barbecue, using indirect heat, following manufacturer's instructions, about 40 minutes or until cooked as desired.

serves 6

per serving 17.7g fat; 1267kJ

lamb and haloumi kebabs

PREPARATION TIME 30 MINUTES ■ COOKING TIME 15 MINUTES

750g diced lamb

200g semi-dried tomatoes

**400g haloumi cheese,
   chopped coarsely**

⅓ cup (80ml) red wine vinegar

2 cloves garlic, crushed

⅓ cup (80ml) olive oil

1 Thread lamb, tomato and cheese onto eight skewers.

2 Place kebabs in shallow dish; pour over combined remaining ingredients. Cover; refrigerate 3 hours or overnight.

3 Drain kebabs; discard marinade. Cook kebabs on heated oiled barbecue until browned all over and cooked as desired.

serves 4

per serving   42.9g fat; 3048kJ

tip   If using bamboo skewers, soak in water for at least 1 hour before using, to avoid scorching.

tandoori lamb cutlets with cucumber salad

PREPARATION TIME 25 MINUTES (plus marinating time) ■ COOKING TIME 15 MINUTES

3/4 cup (210g) yogurt

2 cloves garlic, quartered

1 large brown onion (200g),
 chopped coarsely

2 tablespoons grated fresh ginger

1/4 cup (60ml) lemon juice

1 teaspoon chilli powder

2 teaspoons garam masala

1 tablespoon sweet paprika

2 teaspoons ground cumin

12 lamb cutlets (900g), trimmed

CUCUMBER SALAD

2 small green cucumbers (260g)

2 fresh red thai chillies, seeded,
 chopped finely

1/4 cup (60ml) peanut oil

1 1/2 tablespoons lemon juice

1 clove garlic, crushed

2 teaspoons cumin seeds, toasted

1 tablespoon finely shredded
 fresh mint

CORIANDER YOGURT

1/2 cup loosely packed fresh
 coriander leaves

3/4 cup (210g) yogurt

1 Blend or process yogurt, garlic, onion, ginger, juice and spices until pureed.

2 Pour tandoori marinade over lamb in large bowl; stir to coat well. Cover; refrigerate 3 hours or overnight.

3 Cook undrained lamb on heated oiled barbecue, uncovered, until browned both sides and cooked as desired.

4 Serve lamb with cucumber salad and coriander yogurt.

cucumber salad Using a vegetable peeler, peel cucumbers into long thin ribbons. Just before serving, gently toss cucumber with remaining ingredients in medium bowl.

coriander yogurt Blend or process coriander and yogurt until combined.

serves 4

per serving 28.3g fat; 1817kJ
tip The tandoori marinade can also be used with poultry and seafood. It can be made up to 2 days ahead and refrigerated, covered.

lamb chops with
sun-dried tomato pesto

PREPARATION TIME 15 MINUTES (plus marinating time)
COOKING TIME 15 MINUTES

6 lamb chump chops (660g)
½ cup (125ml) lemon juice
½ cup (125ml) dry white wine
2 cloves garlic, crushed

SUN-DRIED TOMATO PESTO

1 cup (150g) drained sun-dried tomatoes
½ cup (125ml) olive oil
½ cup (80g) pine nuts, toasted
⅓ cup (25g) grated parmesan cheese
2 tablespoons lemon juice
2 cloves garlic, crushed

1 Trim fat from lamb. Place lamb in shallow dish; pour over combined juice, wine and garlic. Cover; refrigerate 3 hours or overnight.

2 Drain lamb; discard marinade.

3 Cook lamb on heated oiled barbecue, uncovered, until browned and cooked as desired.

4 Serve with sun-dried tomato pesto.

sun-dried tomato pesto Blend or process ingredients until combined.

serves 6

per serving 41g fat; 2166kJ

herbed lamb steaks

PREPARATION TIME 10 MINUTES (plus marinating time) ■ COOKING TIME 15 MINUTES

**2 tablespoons finely chopped
fresh oregano**

**2 tablespoons finely chopped
fresh flat-leaf parsley**

**1 tablespoon finely chopped
fresh rosemary**

⅓ cup (80ml) red wine

¼ cup (60ml) olive oil

4 lamb leg steaks (800g)

**1 tablespoon coarsely chopped
fresh flat-leaf parsley, extra**

1 Combine herbs, wine and oil in shallow dish; add lamb. Cover; refrigerate 3 hours or overnight.

2 Cook lamb on heated oiled barbecue, uncovered, until browned and cooked as desired; sprinkle with extra parsley.

serves 4

per serving 20.9g fat; 1525kJ

grilled curried cutlets with tomato chickpea salad

PREPARATION TIME 15 MINUTES (plus marinating time) ■ COOKING TIME 15 MINUTES

12 lamb cutlets (900g), trimmed

⅓ cup (80ml) lime juice

2 cloves garlic

1 teaspoon garam masala

2 teaspoons ground cumin

2 teaspoons ground coriander

2 limes, cut into wedges

TOMATO CHICKPEA SALAD

**2 x 300g cans chickpeas,
   rinsed, drained**

**2 medium tomatoes (380g), seeded,
   chopped finely**

**1 medium red onion (170g),
   chopped finely**

1 tablespoon olive oil

2 tablespoons lemon juice

**1 tablespoon coarsely chopped
   fresh coriander**

1 clove garlic, crushed

1 Toss lamb in large bowl with combined juice, garlic and spices. Cover; refrigerate 3 hours or overnight.

2 Drain lamb; discard marinade.

3 Cook lamb on heated oiled barbecue, uncovered, until browned and cooked as desired.

4 Serve with lime wedges and tomato chickpea salad.

tomato chickpea salad Combine ingredients in medium bowl.

serves 4

per serving 17.6g fat; 1564kJ

minted butterflied leg of lamb

PREPARATION TIME 10 MINUTES (plus marinating time) ■ COOKING TIME 50 MINUTES

1.5kg butterflied leg of lamb
1 cup (250ml) dry white wine
3 cloves garlic, crushed
1/4 cup coarsely chopped fresh mint
1/4 cup coarsely chopped fresh flat-leaf parsley
2 tablespoons soy sauce
1 tablespoon brown sugar

1 Combine lamb with remaining ingredients in disposable baking dish.
Cover; refrigerate 3 hours or overnight.

2 Cook lamb in covered barbecue, using indirect heat, following
manufacturer's instructions, about 50 minutes or until cooked as desired,
turning lamb halfway through cooking and brushing occasionally with
pan juices. Sprinkle with additional mint and parsley, if desired.

serves 6

per serving 15.1g fat; 1661kJ

chorizo pizza

PREPARATION TIME 10 MINUTES
COOKING TIME 10 MINUTES

4 x 112g pizza bases
1/3 cup (80ml) bottled pasta sauce
2 chorizo sausages (260g), sliced thinly
1 medium white onion (150g), sliced thinly
1 medium red capsicum (200g), sliced thinly
1/2 cup (60g) seeded black olives, sliced thickly
2 tablespoons coarsely chopped fresh basil
200g bocconcini cheese, sliced thinly

1 Spread pizza bases with sauce; top with sausage, onion, capsicum, olive, basil and cheese.

2 Cook in covered barbecue, using indirect heat, following manufacturer's instructions, about 10 minutes or until cheese melts.

serves 4

per serving 36.7g fat; 3135kJ

roasted vegetable pizza

PREPARATION TIME 15 MINUTES
COOKING TIME 30 MINUTES

4 baby eggplants (240g), sliced thinly
3 medium zucchini (360g), sliced thinly
4 x 112g pizza bases
1/2 cup (130g) sun-dried tomato pesto
1 medium red capsicum (200g),
  seeded, chopped finely
200g haloumi cheese, sliced thinly

1 Cook eggplant and zucchini on heated oiled barbecue until just tender.

2 Spread pizza bases with pesto; top with eggplant, zucchini, capsicum and cheese.

3 Cook in covered barbecue, using indirect heat, following manufacturer's instructions, about 10 minutes or until cheese melts.

serves 4

per serving 26.2g fat; 2513kJ

three-mushroom pizza

PREPARATION TIME 15 MINUTES
COOKING TIME 10 MINUTES

4 x 112g pizza bases
20g butter, melted
1 clove garlic, crushed
100g button mushrooms, sliced thinly
100g swiss brown mushrooms, sliced thinly
100g oyster mushrooms, halved
**½ cup (60g) coarsely grated smoked
  cheddar cheese**
½ cup (40g) finely grated parmesan cheese
1 cup (125g) coarsely grated cheddar cheese
1 tablespoon finely chopped chives

1 Brush pizza bases with combined butter and garlic;
  top with mushrooms and cheeses.

2 Cook in covered barbecue, using indirect heat,
  following manufacturer's instructions, about
  10 minutes or until cheese melts. Sprinkle
  with chives.

serves 4

per serving 26.5g fat; 2484kJ

satay prawn pizza

PREPARATION TIME 25 MINUTES
COOKING TIME 10 MINUTES

4 x 112g pizza bases
½ cup (125ml) bottled satay marinade
1 medium brown onion (150g), sliced thinly
100g snow peas, sliced thinly
500g small uncooked prawns, shelled
½ cup (75g) roasted cashews
2 tablespoons coarsely chopped fresh coriander
1 cup (125g) pizza cheese

1 Spread pizza bases with marinade; top with
  onion, snow peas, prawns, cashews, coriander
  and cheese.

2 Cook in covered barbecue, using indirect heat,
  following manufacturer's instructions, about
  10 minutes or until cheese melts.

serves 4

per serving 24.4g fat; 2754kJ

pizza

beef & veal

There are a few simple tricks to perfectly barbecued beef
– turn it once only, don't pierce it (or all the juices will escape)
and let it rest afterwards. Cover the meat loosely with foil
then stand it in a warm place, to allow the juices to settle.

beef skewers on lettuce cups

PREPARATION TIME 45 MINUTES (plus marinating time) ■ COOKING TIME 10 MINUTES

500g beef rump steak, sliced thinly

½ telegraph cucumber (200g), peeled, halved then quartered lengthways

6 green onions, cut into 5cm lengths, then into thin strips

1 cup (80g) bean sprouts

1 large carrot (180g), cut into 5cm lengths, then into strips

8 lettuce leaves

MARINADE

2 tablespoons finely chopped fresh lemon grass

1 medium white onion (150g), sliced thinly

2 cloves garlic, crushed

2 teaspoons sugar

2 fresh red thai chillies, seeded, chopped finely

2 teaspoons sesame oil

2 teaspoons sesame seeds

SAUCE

2 cloves garlic, chopped finely

1 fresh red thai chilli, seeded, chopped finely

1 tablespoon sugar

2 tablespoons lime juice

¼ cup (60ml) rice vinegar

¼ cup (60ml) fish sauce

¼ cup (60ml) water

1 Combine beef and marinade in large bowl. Cover; refrigerate 3 hours or overnight.

2 Thread beef onto 16 skewers.

3 Cook beef on heated oiled barbecue, uncovered, until browned and cooked as desired.

4 Divide cucumber, onion, sprouts and carrot among lettuce leaves. Top with beef; drizzle with sauce.

marinade Combine ingredients in small bowl.

sauce Blend or process ingredients until combined.

serves 4

per serving 9.2g fat; 1118kJ
tip If using bamboo skewers, soak in water for at least 1 hour before using, to avoid scorching.

peppered steak sandwich

PREPARATION TIME 20 MINUTES (plus standing time) ■ COOKING TIME 20 MINUTES

400g piece beef fillet

2 tablespoons cracked black pepper

2 teaspoons finely grated lemon rind

6 small tomatoes (780g), halved

8 thick slices grain or brown bread, toasted

2 tablespoons yogurt

2 teaspoons seeded mustard

30g spinach leaves

1 Coat beef in combined pepper and rind.

2 Cook beef on heated oiled barbecue, uncovered, until browned and cooked as desired. Remove from barbecue; stand, covered, 5 minutes.

3 Meanwhile, cook tomato on heated oiled barbecue, uncovered, until browned lightly and slightly softened.

4 Spread toast with combined yogurt and mustard.

5 Cut beef into eight slices. Arrange half of the spinach on toast; top with beef, tomato and remaining spinach.

serves 4

per serving 8g fat; 1565kJ

veal souvlakia with tomato and onion salsa

PREPARATION TIME 40 MINUTES (plus marinating time)
COOKING TIME 10 MINUTES

1kg whole piece veal fillets

4 pitta bread rounds

MARINADE

1 small brown onion (80g), chopped coarsely

2 cloves garlic, crushed

1/4 cup (70g) yogurt

1 tablespoon lemon juice

1 tablespoon olive oil

1/4 cup firmly packed fresh mint leaves

3 teaspoons white wine vinegar

TOMATO AND ONION SALSA

4 medium egg tomatoes (300g), seeded, chopped finely

1 medium white onion (150g), chopped finely

2 tablespoons finely chopped fresh mint

1 teaspoon sweet paprika

YOGURT SAUCE

3/4 cup (210g) yogurt

2 teaspoons tahini

1 tablespoon hot water

1 Cut veal into 3cm pieces; thread onto eight skewers. Combine veal and marinade in large shallow dish. Cover; refrigerate 3 hours or overnight.

2 Cook veal on heated oiled barbecue, uncovered, until browned and cooked as desired.

3 Serve veal with tomato and onion salsa, yogurt sauce and warm pitta bread.

marinade Blend or process ingredients until combined.

tomato and onion salsa Combine ingredients in small bowl.

yogurt sauce Whisk ingredients in small bowl until combined.

serves 4

per serving 16.2g fat; 2581kJ
tip If using bamboo skewers, soak in water for at least 1 hour before using, to avoid scorching.

steaks with capsicum salsa

PREPARATION TIME 20 MINUTES ■ COOKING TIME 10 MINUTES

**1 small red capsicum (150g),
chopped finely**

**1 small green capsicum (150g),
chopped finely**

**1 medium red onion (170g),
chopped finely**

**1 large tomato (250g), seeded,
chopped finely**

**1 tablespoon finely chopped
fresh coriander**

**¼ cup (60ml) bottled
french dressing**

2 cloves garlic, crushed

1 teaspoon ground cumin

4 beef eye fillet steaks (600g)

1 Combine capsicums, onion, tomato, coriander, dressing, garlic and cumin in medium bowl; mix well.

2 Cook beef on heated oiled barbecue, uncovered, until browned and cooked as desired. Serve beef with capsicum salsa.

serves 4

per serving 11.3g fat; 1103kJ

piquant grilled steaks

PREPARATION TIME 5 MINUTES (plus marinating time) ■ COOKING TIME 10 MINUTES

¼ cup (60ml) soy sauce

2 tablespoons oyster sauce

1 tablespoon hoisin sauce

1 tablespoon brown sugar

1 tablespoon dry sherry

1 clove garlic, crushed

1 teaspoon sesame oil

4 beef T-bone steaks (1kg)

1 Combine sauces, sugar, sherry, garlic and oil in large shallow dish; add beef. Cover; refrigerate 3 hours or overnight.

2 Drain beef; reserve marinade.

3 Cook beef on heated oiled barbecue, uncovered, until browned and cooked as desired, brushing with reserved marinade during cooking.

4 Serve beef with salad, if desired.

serves 4

per serving 15g fat; 1288kJ

sweet chilli beef ribs

PREPARATION TIME 10 MINUTES (plus marinating time)
COOKING TIME 30 MINUTES

½ cup (125ml) sweet chilli sauce

1 tablespoon soy sauce

¼ cup (60ml) rice wine

2 cloves garlic, crushed

1 teaspoon grated fresh ginger

2 tablespoons finely chopped fresh coriander

1.5kg beef spare ribs

1 Combine sauces, wine, garlic, ginger and coriander in large shallow dish; add ribs. Cover; refrigerate 3 hours or overnight.

2 Cook ribs in covered barbecue, using indirect heat, following manufacturer's instructions, about 30 minutes or until browned all over and cooked as desired.

serves 4

per serving 11.4g fat; 1206kJ

veal chops with chickpea and tomato salad

PREPARATION TIME 15 MINUTES (plus marinating time) ■ COOKING TIME 10 MINUTES

1 teaspoon ground coriander

1 teaspoon ground cumin

¼ teaspoon chilli powder

2 teaspoons grated lemon rind

1 tablespoon olive oil

4 veal T-bone steaks (750g)

CHICKPEA AND TOMATO SALAD

300g can chickpeas, rinsed, drained

2 large tomatoes (500g), seeded, chopped finely

1 small red onion (100g), chopped finely

2 green onions, chopped finely

2 tablespoons coarsely chopped fresh coriander

1 tablespoon coarsely chopped fresh mint

1 teaspoon grated lemon rind

¼ cup (60ml) lemon juice

⅓ cup (80ml) olive oil

1 Combine spices, rind and oil in large bowl; add veal. Cover; refrigerate 3 hours or overnight.

2 Cook cutlets on heated oiled barbecue, uncovered, until browned and cooked as desired. Serve with chickpea and tomato salad.

chickpea and tomato salad Combine ingredients in medium bowl.

serves 4

per serving 27.7g fat; 1739kJ

beef and onion kebabs

PREPARATION TIME 20 MINUTES (plus marinating time)   COOKING TIME 10 MINUTES

700g beef rump steak

18 baby onions (450g), halved

MARINADE

½ cup (125ml) tomato sauce

½ cup (175g) honey

½ cup (125ml) lemon juice

2 tablespoons finely chopped fresh oregano

1 tablespoon grated fresh ginger

1 tablespoon worcestershire sauce

1 Cut beef into 3cm pieces.

2 Thread beef and onion onto 12 skewers.

3 Place kebabs in shallow dish; add marinade. Cover; refrigerate 3 hours or overnight.

4 Cook kebabs on heated oiled barbecue, uncovered, until browned and cooked as desired.

marinade Combine ingredients in medium jug.

serves 4

per serving 8.3g fat; 1872kJ

tip If using bamboo skewers, soak in water for at least 1 hour before using, to avoid scorching.

thai-style steaks
with cucumber salad

PREPARATION TIME 25 MINUTES (plus marinating time)
COOKING TIME 15 MINUTES

Beef rib-eye steak is also called scotch fillet by some butchers.

6 beef rib-eye steaks (900g)
1/4 cup (60ml) mild sweet chilli sauce
2 cloves garlic, crushed
2 teaspoons fish sauce
1/4 cup (60ml) lime juice
2 tablespoons coarsely chopped fresh coriander

CUCUMBER SALAD
3 small lebanese cucumbers (390g)
1/3 cup (75g) caster sugar
2/3 cup (160ml) white vinegar
1 fresh red thai chilli, seeded, sliced thinly
1/4 cup (35g) chopped, unsalted, roasted peanuts
1 tablespoon coarsely chopped fresh coriander

1 Combine beef with remaining ingredients in shallow
dish. Cover; refrigerate 3 hours or overnight.

2 Drain beef; discard marinade.

3 Cook beef on heated oiled barbecue, uncovered,
until browned and cooked as desired.

4 Serve beef with drained cucumber salad.

cucumber salad Halve cucumbers lengthways.
Scoop out and discard seeds; slice cucumber thinly.
Combine sugar and vinegar in medium saucepan;
stir over heat, without boiling, until sugar dissolves.
Simmer, uncovered, about 5 minutes or until reduced
to 1/2 cup (125ml). Combine hot vinegar mixture
with cucumber and remaining ingredients in heatproof
bowl; mix well. Cover; refrigerate 3 hours or overnight.

serves 6

per serving 12.5g fat; 1312kJ

mustard T-bone with jacket potato

PREPARATION TIME 10 MINUTES ■ COOKING TIME 1 HOUR 10 MINUTES

8 medium potatoes (1.6kg)

8 beef T-bone steaks (2kg)

1/3 cup (95g) dijon mustard

**1/3 cup coarsely chopped fresh
flat-leaf parsley**

**1/4 cup coarsely chopped
fresh rosemary**

1 Wrap potatoes individually in foil; place in disposable baking dish. Cook in covered barbecue, using indirect heat, following manufacturer's instructions, about 1 hour or until tender.

2 Brush beef all over with mustard; cook on heated oiled barbecue, uncovered, until browned and cooked as desired. Sprinkle with combined herbs.

3 Serve beef with potato.

serves 8

per serving 8.7g fat; 1456kJ

tandoori beef with grilled limes

PREPARATION TIME 10 MINUTES (plus marinating time) ■ COOKING TIME 10 MINUTES

Beef rib-eye steak is also called scotch fillet by some butchers.

4 beef rib-eye steaks (600g)
1 clove garlic, crushed
1/4 cup (75g) tandoori paste
4 limes, halved
1/2 cup (160g) mango chutney
3/4 cup (210g) yogurt

1 Combine beef, garlic and paste in large bowl. Cover; refrigerate 3 hours or overnight.

2 Cook beef on heated oiled barbecue, uncovered, until browned and cooked as desired.

3 Meanwhile, cook lime on heated oiled barbecue plate; cook about 2 minutes or until browned.

4 Serve beef with lime, chutney and yogurt; accompany with steamed beans and saffron rice, if desired.

serves 4

per serving 17.1g fat; 1641kJ

spicy veal cutlets

PREPARATION TIME 5 MINUTES (plus marinating time)
COOKING TIME 10 MINUTES

2 tablespoons oyster sauce

1 tablespoon fish sauce

1 tablespoon tamarind sauce

2 tablespoons peanut oil

2 teaspoons ground cumin

2 teaspoons ground coriander

1/4 teaspoon chilli powder

1 tablespoon sambal oelek

2 cloves garlic, crushed

6 veal cutlets (900g)

1 Combine sauces, oil, spices, sambal oelek and garlic
   in shallow dish; add veal. Cover; refrigerate 3 hours
   or overnight.

2 Cook cutlets on heated oiled barbecue, uncovered,
   until browned and cooked as desired.

serves 6

per serving 9.3g fat; 841kJ

teriyaki beef kebabs

PREPARATION TIME 20 MINUTES (plus marinating time) ■ COOKING TIME 15 MINUTES

**800g beef rump steaks,
  chopped coarsely**

**2 medium brown onions (300g),
  chopped coarsely**

MARINADE

1 cup (250ml) teriyaki marinade

2 cloves garlic, crushed

1 tablespoon grated fresh ginger

1 tablespoon peanut oil

2 teaspoons lemon juice

1 Combine beef and marinade in large bowl. Cover; refrigerate 3 hours or overnight.

2 Thread beef and onion, alternately, onto eight bamboo skewers. Cook kebabs on heated oiled barbecue, uncovered, until browned and cooked as desired.

marinade Combine ingredients in medium bowl; mix well.

serves 4

per serving 13.9g fat; 1624kJ

tip If using bamboo skewers, soak in water for at least 1 hour before using, to avoid scorching.

beef fajitas

PREPARATION TIME 30 MINUTES (plus marinating time) ■ COOKING TIME 10 MINUTES

⅓ cup (80ml) barbecue sauce

1 teaspoon ground cumin

1 teaspoon ground coriander

½ teaspoon chilli powder

500g beef fillet, sliced thinly

1 small red capsicum (150g),
   seeded, sliced thinly

1 small green capsicum (150g),
   seeded, sliced thinly

1 small yellow capsicum (150g),
   seeded, sliced thinly

8 large flour tortillas

¾ cup (180g) sour cream

AVOCADO TOPPING

2 medium avocados (500g)

1 tablespoon lime juice

1 clove garlic, crushed

TOMATO SALSA

2 medium tomatoes (380g), seeded,
   chopped finely

1 small red onion (100g),
   chopped finely

1 tablespoon olive oil

2 teaspoons finely chopped
   fresh coriander

1 Combine sauce and spices in medium bowl; add beef. Cover;
   refrigerate 3 hours or overnight.

2 Cook beef and capsicums on heated oiled barbecue, uncovered,
   until beef is browned and capsicums are tender.

3 Meanwhile, wrap tortillas in foil, in parcels of four, and heat on barbecue.
   Remove tortillas from foil and divide beef mixture among them. Top with
   sour cream, avocado topping and tomato salsa; roll to enclose filling.

avocado topping Mash avocado coarsely in medium bowl with fork;
mash in lime juice and garlic.

tomato salsa Combine ingredients in small bowl.

serves 4

per serving 53.3g fat; 3462kJ

balsamic and ginger beef

PREPARATION TIME 10 MINUTES (plus marinating time) ■ COOKING TIME 10 MINUTES

½ cup (125ml) olive oil
¼ cup (60ml) balsamic vinegar
1 tablespoon grated fresh ginger
1 teaspoon brown sugar
1 teaspoon soy sauce
4 beef T-bone steaks (1kg)

1 Combine oil, vinegar, ginger, sugar and sauce in screw-top jar; shake well. Reserve ¼ cup (60ml) of the vinegar mixture; brush beef all over using about half of the remaining mixture. Cover; refrigerate 3 hours or overnight.

2 Cook beef on heated oiled barbecue, uncovered, until browned and cooked as desired, brushing beef occasionally with remaining vinegar mixture during cooking.

3 Pour reserved vinegar mixture over beef. Serve with salad, if desired.

serves 4

per serving 37.3g fat; 1967kJ

veal cutlets in maple marinade

PREPARATION TIME 5 MINUTES (plus marinating time) ■ COOKING TIME 10 MINUTES

1½ cups (375ml) tomato sauce
1 tablespoon soy sauce
½ cup (175g) maple syrup
6 veal cutlets (900g)

1 Combine sauces and syrup in large shallow dish; add veal. Cover; refrigerate 3 hours or overnight.

2 Drain veal; reserve marinade.

3 Cook veal on heated oiled barbecue, uncovered, until browned and cooked as desired, brushing with reserved marinade during cooking.

serves 6

per serving 2.9g fat; 1125kJ

beef spare ribs

PREPARATION TIME 10 MINUTES (plus marinating time) ■ COOKING TIME 20 MINUTES

2 cups (500ml) tomato sauce

½ cup (125ml) worcestershire sauce

¾ cup (180ml) vegetable oil

½ cup (125ml) water

¼ cup (60ml) white vinegar

⅓ cup (75g) firmly packed brown sugar

1 medium brown onion (150g), chopped finely

1.5kg beef spare ribs

1 Combine sauces, oil, the water, vinegar, sugar and onion in large shallow dish; add ribs. Cover; refrigerate 3 hours or overnight.

2 Drain ribs; reserve marinade.

3 Place reserved marinade in small saucepan; bring to a boil. Reduce heat; simmer, uncovered, until thickened slightly.

4 Cook ribs on heated oiled barbecue, uncovered, until browned and cooked through. Pour sauce over ribs. Serve with salad, if desired.

serves 4

per serving 54.1g fat; 3999kJ

steak and aïoli
open sandwiches

PREPARATION TIME 15 MINUTES ■ COOKING TIME 10 MINUTES

Beef sirloin, rib-eye or rump are suitable for this recipe.
Ciabatta is a type of crusty Italian bread.

8 thin beef fillet steaks (800g)
4 large egg tomatoes (360g), halved
1 tablespoon olive oil
½ cup (150g) mayonnaise
1 clove garlic, crushed
4 slices ciabatta
1 tablespoon finely shredded fresh basil
1 tablespoon balsamic vinegar

1 Cook beef and tomato on heated oiled barbecue,
uncovered, until beef is browned and cooked as
desired. Drizzle tomato with oil; cook until tender.

2 Combine mayonnaise and garlic in small bowl.

3 Toast bread; spread with mayonnaise mixture. Top with
beef and tomato; sprinkle with basil and vinegar. Serve
with salad greens, if desired.

serves 4

per serving 27.2g fat; 2178kJ

port-smoked beef

PREPARATION TIME 10 MINUTES (plus marinating time) ■ COOKING TIME 1 HOUR 35 MINUTES

You need 250g smoking chips for this recipe.

2 tablespoons olive oil

2 cloves garlic, crushed

¼ cup (60ml) port

2 tablespoons coarsely chopped fresh oregano

1.5kg beef fillet

1 cup (250ml) port, extra

1 Combine oil, garlic, port and oregano in large bowl; add beef. Cover; refrigerate 3 hours or overnight.

2 Combine smoking chips and extra port in small bowl. Cover; stand 3 hours or overnight.

3 Cook beef on heated oiled barbecue, uncovered, until just browned all over. Place beef in disposable baking dish. Place drained smoking chips in smoke box; place beside beef on barbecue.

4 Cook in covered barbecue, using indirect heat, following manufacturer's instructions, 1½ hours or until cooked as desired.

serves 8

per serving 13.6g fat; 1224kJ

thai beef salad

PREPARATION TIME 30 MINUTES (plus marinating time) ■ COOKING TIME 10 MINUTES (plus standing time)

800g beef rump steak

2 tablespoons fish sauce

1/3 cup (80ml) lime juice

1/3 cup (80ml) peanut oil

2 tablespoons brown sugar

2 cloves garlic, crushed

1 lebanese cucumber (130g)

3 1/2 cups (200g) snow pea sprouts

6 green onions, chopped finely

2 1/2 cups (200g) bean sprouts

**1/2 cup loosely packed fresh
    purple basil leaves**

**1/2 cup loosely packed fresh
    thai basil leaves**

4 fresh red thai chillies, sliced thinly

500g radishes, sliced thinly

1 Combine beef and half of the combined sauce, juice, oil, sugar and garlic in large bowl. Cover; refrigerate 3 hours or overnight.

2 Using vegetable peeler, slice cucumber into thin ribbons.

3 Drain beef; discard marinade. Cook beef on heated oiled barbecue until browned all over and cooked as desired. Stand 5 minutes; slice thinly.

4 Just before serving, combine beef, reserved sauce mixture, cucumber and remaining ingredients in large bowl; toss gently.

serves 6

per serving 13.6g fat; 1224kJ

rib steaks with capsicum pesto and mashed kumara

PREPARATION TIME 40 MINUTES ■ COOKING TIME 30 MINUTES

4 beef rib steaks (1.2kg), with bone in

CAPSICUM PESTO
2 large red capsicums (700g), seeded, quartered
1/2 cup (75g) sun-dried tomatoes in oil, drained
1 tablespoon grated fresh ginger
1 tablespoon olive oil
1 teaspoon sugar
2 tablespoons finely chopped fresh basil

MASHED KUMARA
2 large kumara (1kg), chopped coarsely
1 large potato (300g), chopped coarsely
1/4 cup (60ml) cream
1 clove garlic, crushed
1 teaspoon ground cumin

1 Cook beef on heated oiled barbecue, uncovered, until browned and cooked as desired.

2 Serve steaks, topped with capsicum pesto, on mashed kumara.

capsicum pesto Blend or process capsicum until almost smooth. Strain; discard liquid. Blend or process tomatoes, ginger, oil and sugar. Place mixture in medium bowl; stir in capsicum puree and basil.

mashed kumara Boil, steam or microwave kumara and potato, until tender; drain. Mash together with cream, garlic and cumin.

serves 4

per serving 28.5g fat; 2971kJ

peppered beef

PREPARATION TIME 10 MINUTES ■ COOKING TIME 20 MINUTES

½ cup (70g) cracked black pepper

1kg piece beef eye fillet

3 medium green zucchini (360g), sliced thinly

3 medium yellow zucchini (360g), sliced thinly

1 Press pepper onto side of beef.

2 Cut beef into six pieces.

3 Cook beef and zucchini on heated oiled barbecue until zucchini is tender and beef is browned all over and cooked as desired.

serves 6

per serving 8.6g fat; 1063kJ

balsamic beef with grilled eggplant

PREPARATION TIME 25 MINUTES (plus marinating and standing time) ■ COOKING TIME 20 MINUTES

Beef rib-eye steak is also called scotch fillet by some butchers.

½ cup (125ml) olive oil
⅓ cup (80ml) balsamic vinegar
2 cloves garlic, crushed
6 beef rib-eye steaks (900g)
2 medium eggplants (600g),
   chopped coarsely
2 teaspoons salt
500g cherry tomatoes
150g baby rocket leaves

1 Combine oil, vinegar and garlic in medium jug.

2 Pour half of the vinegar mixture over beef in large bowl. Cover; refrigerate 3 hours or overnight.

3 Place eggplant in colander. Sprinkle with salt; stand 10 minutes. Rinse under cold water; drain on absorbent paper.

4 Drain beef; discard marinade.

5 Cook beef, eggplant and tomatoes on heated oiled barbecue, uncovered, until beef is browned and cooked as desired, and eggplant and tomato are tender.

6 Combine eggplant, tomato, rocket and remaining balsamic mixture in large bowl. Serve beef with eggplant mixture.

serves 6

per serving 28.6g fat; 1683kJ

mediterranean steak towers

PREPARATION TIME 30 MINUTES (plus standing time)
COOKING TIME 25 MINUTES

1 large red capsicum (350g)
1 large eggplant (500g), sliced thinly
2 medium zucchini (240g), sliced thinly, lengthways
2 tablespoons olive oil
4 beef fillet steaks (900g)
40cm loaf turkish bread
30g mesclun

BALSAMIC DRESSING
1/3 cup (80ml) olive oil
2 tablespoons balsamic vinegar

1 Quarter capsicum; remove seeds and membranes. Cook capsicum, skin-side down, on heated oiled barbecue, uncovered, until skin blisters and blackens. Cover capsicum pieces with plastic or paper for 5 minutes. Peel away skin; slice capsicum thinly. Cover to keep warm.

2 Brush eggplant and zucchini with oil. Cook on heated oiled barbecue, uncovered, until browned and tender; keep warm.

3 Pound each steak with a meat mallet until an even thickness. Cook steaks on heated oiled barbecue, uncovered, until browned and cooked as desired.

4 Meanwhile, cut bread into four pieces; toast bread.

5 Top toast with mesclun, eggplant, steak, zucchini and capsicum. Drizzle with balsamic dressing.

balsamic dressing Combine oil and vinegar in screw-top jar; shake well.

serves 4

per serving 41g fat; 3247kJ
tip Beef rump, boneless sirloin and rib-eye steaks are also suitable for this recipe.

veal roll-up

PREPARATION TIME 15 MINUTES ■ COOKING TIME 10 MINUTES

4 veal steaks (400g)

¼ cup (35g) plain flour

1 egg, beaten lightly

1 cup (100g) packaged breadcrumbs

**2 medium avocados (500g),
   sliced thinly**

2 cups (110g) snow pea sprouts

4 pieces lavash bread

½ cup (125ml) sweet chilli sauce

1 Using a meat mallet, pound veal until even thickness.

2 Dip veal in flour; shake off excess. Dip in egg then coat in breadcrumbs.

3 Cook veal on heated oiled barbecue plate, uncovered, until browned all over and cooked through.

4 Divide veal, avocado and sprouts among bread. Drizzle with sauce; roll to enclose.

serves 4

per serving 26.9g fat; 2857kJ

steak with herb vinaigrette

PREPARATION TIME 20 MINUTES (plus marinating time) ■ COOKING TIME 10 MINUTES (plus standing time)

½ cup (125ml) dry red wine

2 tablespoons olive oil

1 clove garlic, crushed

500g beef rump steak

4 pitta pocket breads

80g baby rocket leaves

2 medium tomatoes (260g), sliced thinly

1 lebanese cucumber (130g), sliced thinly

HERB VINAIGRETTE

¼ cup coarsely chopped fresh flat-leaf parsley

2 teaspoons coarsely chopped fresh rosemary

⅓ cup (80ml) olive oil

2 tablespoons red wine vinegar

¼ teaspoon sugar

1 small red onion (100g), chopped finely

1 Combine wine, oil and garlic in large bowl; add beef. Cover; refrigerate 3 hours or overnight.

2 Drain beef; discard marinade.

3 Cook beef on heated oiled barbecue, uncovered, until browned and cooked as desired. Cover; stand 5 minutes before slicing thinly.

4 Split bread open; fill with rocket, tomato, cucumber, beef and herb vinaigrette.

herb vinaigrette Combine ingredients in medium jug.

serves 4

per serving 34.2g fat; 2385kJ

balsamic vinegar marinade

PREPARATION TIME 5 MINUTES

One quantity of balsamic vinegar marinade is enough for about 1kg of chicken, beef, lamb or baby octopus. It can be made 3 days ahead and refrigerated, covered.

¼ cup (60ml) lemon juice
2 tablespoons olive oil
¼ cup (60ml) balsamic vinegar
2 cloves garlic, crushed
3 teaspoons brown sugar
2 teaspoons finely chopped fresh thyme

1 Combine ingredients in medium jug.

makes ³/₄ cup

per quantity 36.7g fat; 1623kJ

red wine marinade

PREPARATION TIME 5 MINUTES

One quantity of red wine marinade is enough for about 1kg lamb, beef or veal. It can be made 3 days ahead and refrigerated, covered.

½ cup (125ml) dry red wine
2 teaspoons dijon mustard
1 clove garlic, crushed
½ teaspoon finely chopped fresh thyme

1 Combine ingredients in medium jug.

makes ¹/₂ cup

per quantity 0.3g fat; 382kJ

honey soy marinade

PREPARATION TIME 5 MINUTES

One quantity of honey soy marinade is enough for about 1kg beef, pork or lamb. It can be made 3 days ahead and refrigerated, covered.

1 tablespoon honey, warmed
1/3 cup (80ml) soy sauce
1 teaspoon sesame oil
2 cloves garlic, crushed
2 teaspoons grated fresh ginger

1 Combine ingredients in small jug.

makes 1/2 cup

per quantity 4.8g fat; 710kJ

yogurt marinade

PREPARATION TIME 5 MINUTES

One quantity of yogurt marinade in enough for about 1kg lamb or chicken. It can be made a day ahead and refrigerated, covered.

1/2 cup (140g) yogurt
1 clove garlic, crushed
1 fresh red thai chilli, seeded, chopped finely
1/2 teaspoon sweet paprika
2 teaspoons finely chopped fresh mint

1 Combine ingredients in small bowl.

makes 1/2 cup

per quantity 5g fat; 451kJ

pork

Pork is the other great white meat. Suitable for both covered
and uncovered barbecue varieties, fruity-glazed roast loin,
steaks and marinated kebabs are favourites, but
best of all are succulent pork spare ribs.

spiced pork skewers with honey glaze

PREPARATION TIME 15 MINUTES ■ COOKING TIME 15 MINUTES

500g pork fillets
2 cloves garlic, crushed
2 teaspoons cumin seeds
½ teaspoon ground coriander
¼ teaspoon sweet paprika
1 tablespoon olive oil

HONEY GLAZE
½ cup (125ml) orange juice
2 tablespoons honey
2 tablespoons barbecue sauce
1 teaspoon dijon mustard

1 Cut pork into 3cm cubes. Combine pork with garlic, cumin, coriander, paprika and oil in medium bowl.

2 Thread pork onto eight skewers.

3 Cook pork on heated oiled barbecue, uncovered, until browned and cooked through. Serve with honey glaze.

honey glaze Combine ingredients in small saucepan; stir over heat until boiling. Reduce heat to low; simmer about 5 minutes or until thickened.

makes 8

per skewer 2.6g fat; 357kJ
tip If using bamboo skewers, soak in water for at least 1 hour before using, to avoid scorching.

salt-rubbed roasted pork loin with sage

PREPARATION TIME 15 MINUTES (plus standing time) ■ COOKING TIME 1 HOUR

10 fresh sage leaves

1kg pork loin (crackling and fat removed)

2 tablespoons sea salt

2 tablespoons crushed dried green peppercorns

2 tablespoons coarsely chopped fresh sage

1 tablespoon olive oil

1 Lay sage leaves in the middle of pork loin; roll pork to enclose leaves. Tie pork at 10cm intervals with kitchen string.

2 Combine salt, peppercorns and chopped sage in small bowl.

3 Brush pork with oil; rub salt mixture over pork.

4 Place pork in disposable baking dish. Cook pork in covered barbecue, using indirect heat, following manufacturer's instructions, about 1 hour or until cooked through.

5 Cover with foil; stand 10 minutes before slicing.

serves 6

per serving 9.4g fat; 970kJ

chinese marinated pork

PREPARATION TIME 15 MINUTES (plus marinating time)
COOKING TIME 15 MINUTES

1kg piece pork neck

MARINADE
2 star anise, crushed
2 tablespoons light soy sauce
2 tablespoons brown sugar
1½ tablespoons honey
1½ tablespoons dry sherry
2 teaspoons hoisin sauce
2 teaspoons grated fresh ginger
1 clove garlic, crushed
2 green onions, chopped finely
red food colouring

1 Cut pork into quarters lengthways. Combine pork and marinade in large shallow dish. Cover; refrigerate 3 hours or overnight.

2 Drain pork; reserve marinade.

3 Cook pork on heated oiled barbecue, uncovered, until browned and cooked through, brushing with reserved marinade during cooking.

marinade Combine ingredients in small bowl.

serves 6

per serving 6.5g fat; 1051kJ

indian pork kebabs with mango chutney

PREPARATION TIME 45 MINUTES (plus marinating time) ■ COOKING TIME 15 MINUTES

1kg pork fillets

¼ cup (75g) madras curry paste

¾ cup (210g) yogurt

2 tablespoons lemon juice

2 large red capsicums (700g)

2 large brown onions (400g)

1 cup (320g) mango chutney

1 Cut pork into 2cm cubes. Whisk paste, yogurt and juice in medium bowl until smooth; add pork. Cover; refrigerate 3 hours or overnight.

2 Cut capsicums into 4cm pieces; cut onions into wedges.

3 Thread pork, capsicum and onion onto 12 skewers.

4 Cook kebabs on heated oiled barbecue, uncovered, until browned and cooked through.

5 Serve kebabs with mango chutney and seasoned rice, if desired.

serves 6

per serving 9.3g fat; 1624kJ

tip If using bamboo skewers, soak in water for at least 1 hour before using, to avoid scorching.

sticky pork ribs

PREPARATION TIME 10 MINUTES (plus marinating time) ■ COOKING TIME 45 MINUTES

2 tablespoons tomato paste

2 tablespoons tomato sauce

2 tablespoons soy sauce

1 teaspoon grated lemon rind

¼ cup (60ml) lemon juice

1 tablespoon brown sugar

1 teaspoon cracked black pepper

1 teaspoon ground allspice

¼ teaspoon chilli powder

2 cloves garlic, crushed

2kg american-style pork spare ribs

1 Combine paste, sauces, rind, juice, sugar, pepper, allspice, chilli powder and garlic in large shallow dish; add pork. Cover; refrigerate 3 hours or overnight.

2 Remove ribs from marinade; reserve marinade.

3 Place ribs in disposable baking dish. Cook ribs in covered barbecue, using indirect heat, following manufacturer's instructions, about 45 minutes or until ribs are cooked through, brushing ribs occasionally with reserved marinade during cooking.

serves 4

per serving 30.4g fat; 1968kJ

spicy pork kebabs

PREPARATION TIME 35 MINUTES (plus marinating time)
COOKING TIME 15 MINUTES

750g pork fillets
6 cloves garlic, crushed
1 tablespoon ground cumin
2 teaspoons ground coriander
2 teaspoons hot paprika
¼ cup coarsely chopped fresh flat-leaf parsley
2 tablespoons coarsely chopped fresh oregano
½ cup (125ml) olive oil

1 Cut pork into 3cm cubes. Combine remaining
  ingredients in large bowl; add pork. Cover;
  refrigerate 3 hours or overnight.

2 Drain pork; discard marinade.

3 Thread pork onto 12 skewers.

4 Cook pork on heated oiled barbecue, uncovered,
  until browned and cooked through. Serve
  with rice and barbecued lime halves,
  if desired.

makes 12

per kebab 11.1g fat; 656kJ
tip If using bamboo skewers, soak in water for at least
1 hour before using, to avoid scorching.

tex-mex ribs

PREPARATION TIME 5 MINUTES (plus marinating time) ■ COOKING TIME 45 MINUTES

1 cup (250ml) barbecue sauce
2 teaspoons chilli powder
2 x 35g packets taco seasoning
2kg american-style pork spare ribs

1 Combine sauce, chilli powder and seasoning in large shallow dish; add ribs. Cover; refrigerate 3 hours or overnight.

2 Place ribs in disposable baking dish. Cook in covered barbecue, using indirect heat, following manufacturer's instructions, about 45 minutes or until ribs are cooked through, brushing ribs occasionally with pan juices during cooking.

serves 4

per serving   31.2g fat; 2455kJ

honey mustard glazed ribs

PREPARATION TIME 10 MINUTES (plus marinating time) ■ COOKING TIME 45 MINUTES

½ cup (125ml) orange juice
½ cup (175g) honey
½ cup (125ml) barbecue sauce
2 tablespoons soy sauce
1 tablespoon seeded mustard
3 cloves garlic, crushed
2kg american-style pork spare ribs

1 Combine juice, honey, sauces, mustard and garlic in large shallow dish; add pork. Cover; refrigerate 3 hours or overnight.

2 Drain pork; reserve marinade.

3 Place ribs in disposable baking dish. Cook ribs in covered barbecue, using indirect heat, following manufacturer's instructions, about 45 minutes or until cooked through, brushing ribs occasionally with reserved marinade during cooking. Sprinkle with orange rind and coriander, if desired.

serves 4

per serving 30.4g fat; 2705kJ

hoisin pork kebabs

PREPARATION TIME 35 MINUTES (plus marinating time)
COOKING TIME 15 MINUTES

½ cup (125ml) hoisin sauce
2 tablespoons plum sauce
2 cloves garlic, crushed
750g pork fillet, sliced thinly
2 green onions
1 small green cucumber

1 Combine sauces and garlic in large bowl; add pork. Cover; refrigerate 3 hours or overnight. Thread pork onto 12 skewers.

2 Cook pork on heated oiled barbecue, uncovered, until browned and cooked through.

3 Meanwhile, thinly slice onions diagonally. Halve cucumber lengthways; discard seeds. Thinly slice cucumber lengthways.

4 Serve pork with onion, cucumber and extra plum sauce, if desired.

serves 4

per serving 6.3g fat; 1273kJ
tip If using bamboo skewers, soak in water for at least 1 hour before using, to avoid scorching.

pork and mandarin salad

PREPARATION TIME 25 MINUTES (plus marinating time) ■ COOKING TIME 1 HOUR (plus standing time)

1kg piece pork neck

2 star anise, crushed

2 tablespoons soy sauce

2 tablespoons brown sugar

1 tablespoon honey

1 tablespoon dry sherry

1 tablespoon hoisin sauce

1 tablespoon grated fresh ginger

1 clove garlic, crushed

few drops red food colouring

565g can lychees in syrup, drained

2 medium mandarins (400g), segmented

4 green onions, sliced thinly

½ cup (75g) raw cashews, toasted

2½ cups (200g) bean sprouts

1 Place pork in shallow dish; pour over combined star anise, soy sauce, sugar, honey, sherry, hoisin sauce, ginger, garlic and colouring. Cover; refrigerate 3 hours or overnight.

2 Drain pork; discard marinade.

3 Place pork in disposable baking dish; cook in covered barbecue, using indirect heat, following manufacturer's instructions about 1 hour or until cooked through. Stand 5 minutes before slicing.

4 Combine remaining ingredients on serving plate; top with pork.

serves 6

per serving 13g fat; 1657kJ

pork with caramelised pineapple

PREPARATION TIME 15 MINUTES (plus marinating time) ■ COOKING TIME 10 MINUTES

1 tablespoon grated fresh ginger

½ cup (125ml) pineapple juice

½ cup (125ml) green ginger wine

⅓ cup (115g) honey

2 tablespoons vegetable oil

8 pork butterfly steaks (1kg)

½ medium pineapple (600g), halved, sliced thickly

1 Combine ginger, juice, wine, honey and oil in jug.

2 Trim excess fat from pork. Place pork in shallow dish; pour over ginger mixture. Cover; refrigerate 3 hours or overnight.

3 Drain pork; reserve marinade.

4 Cook pork and pineapple on heated oiled barbecue, uncovered, until pork is browned and cooked through, brushing occasionally with reserved marinade during cooking. Serve with salad, if desired.

serves 4

per serving 18.1g fat; 2280kJ

orange-glazed ham

PREPARATION TIME 40 MINUTES (plus cooling time)
COOKING TIME 2 HOURS 45 MINUTES

6kg cooked leg of ham
2 small oranges (360g), halved, sliced thinly
whole cloves

ORANGE GLAZE
1/2 cup (170g) orange marmalade
3/4 cup (180ml) orange juice
1/4 cup (50g) firmly packed brown sugar
2 teaspoons dijon mustard
2 tablespoons Cointreau

1 Make a decorative cut through ham rind about
10cm from the shank end of leg. Make a shallow
cut down centre of ham from one end to the other.

2 Place ham in disposable baking dish. Cook in
covered barbecue, using indirect heat, following
manufacturer's instructions, about 45 minutes or
until skin begins to split.

3 Remove from barbecue; cool 15 minutes. Peel
skin away from ham carefully, leaving shank end
intact; discard skin. Do not cut through surface
of top fat, or fat will spread during cooking.
Secure orange slices with cloves in decorative
pattern on ham.

4 Wrap shank in foil; brush ham with orange glaze.
Cook, covered, brushing occasionally with glaze,
about 2 hours or until orange slices are lightly
caramelised and ham is heated through.

orange glaze Mix ingredients in small saucepan;
stir over low heat until marmalade melts.

serves 12

per serving 28.2g fat; 2513kJ
tip Grand Marnier can be substituted for the Cointreau in
this recipe.

sausages & burgers

No wonder mince is our favourite meat! Nothing beats a barbecued sausage – unless it's a juicy hamburger dripping with tomato sauce. Casual food like sausages and burgers are among the best dishes to cook on a barbecue.

mexican burgers

PREPARATION TIME 20 MINUTES ■ COOKING TIME 10 MINUTES

750g minced beef

**310g can red kidney beans,
rinsed, drained**

4 green onions, chopped finely

**2 fresh red thai chillies, seeded,
chopped finely**

1 teaspoon hot paprika

1 tablespoon tomato paste

6 hamburger buns

6 butter lettuce leaves

1 small avocado (200g), mashed

½ cup (120g) sour cream

2 tablespoons lemon juice

1 Combine beef, beans, onion, chilli, paprika and paste in medium bowl. Using hands, shape mixture into six patties.

2 Cook patties on heated oiled barbecue, uncovered, until well browned and cooked through.

3 Split buns in half. Place cut-side down onto barbecue; cook until lightly toasted.

4 Top base of buns with lettuce, patties and combined avocado, sour cream, and juice. Replace top of buns, if desired

serves 6

per serving 26.9g fat; 209kJ

sausage and caramelised onion hot dogs

PREPARATION TIME 10 MINUTES ■ COOKING TIME 20 MINUTES

25g butter

2 large brown onions (400g), sliced thinly

1 clove garlic, crushed

1 tablespoon brown sugar

2 teaspoons balsamic vinegar

1 tablespoon beef stock

4 thin continental sausages

4 hot dog buns

⅓ cup (80ml) tomato sauce

1 Melt butter in medium frying pan on barbecue; cook onion and garlic, stirring, until onion is soft and browned. Add sugar, vinegar and stock; cook, stirring, until thick and syrupy.

2 Meanwhile, cook sausages on heated oiled barbecue until browned and cooked through.

3 Split each bun in half; fill with a sausage, caramelised onion and tomato sauce.

serves 4

per serving 14g fat; 1524kJ

sausages with tomato relish

PREPARATION TIME 10 MINUTES ■ COOKING TIME 30 MINUTES

1 tablespoon olive oil
1 clove garlic, crushed
1 large brown onion (200g), chopped finely
4 large tomatoes (1kg), chopped coarsely
2 tablespoons balsamic vinegar
3 teaspoons brown sugar
2 tablespoons torn fresh basil leaves
20 long, thin sausages

1 Heat oil in medium saucepan; cook garlic and onion, stirring, until browned lightly. Add tomato, vinegar and sugar; simmer, uncovered, stirring occasionally, about 30 minutes or until mixture is reduced by half. Just before serving, add basil.

2 Meanwhile, cook sausages on heated oiled barbecue, uncovered, until browned and cooked through.

3 Serve sausages with warm tomato relish. Sprinkle with extra basil leaves, if desired.

serves 10

per serving 31.4g fat; 1530kJ
tip Tomato relish can be made 2 days ahead and refrigerated, covered; reheat just before serving.

lamb and burghul sausages

PREPARATION TIME 30 MINUTES (plus standing and refrigeration time) ■ COOKING TIME 10 MINUTES

½ cup (80g) burghul

750g minced lamb

¼ cup finely chopped fresh
   flat-leaf parsley

2 tablespoons finely chopped
   fresh mint

1 tablespoon grated lemon rind

2 medium tomatoes (380g), peeled,
   chopped finely

1 tablespoon ground cumin

1 tablespoon ground coriander

2 cloves garlic, crushed

½ cup (35g) stale breadcrumbs

1 egg, beaten lightly

2 large brown onions (400g),
   sliced thinly

1 cup (240g) sour cream

1 Place burghul in small bowl; cover with cold water. Stand 15 minutes; drain.

2 Rinse burghul under cold water; drain. Squeeze to remove excess moisture.

3 Combine burghul in large bowl with lamb, herbs, rind, tomato, cumin, coriander, garlic, breadcrumbs and egg. Using hands, shape ¼-cup measures of the mixture into sausages. Cover; refrigerate 3 hours or overnight.

4 Cook sausages on heated oiled barbecue, uncovered, until browned all over and cooked through.

5 Meanwhile, cook onion on heated barbecue until browned. Serve sausages with onion and sour cream. Accompany with bread and mixed lettuce leaves, if desired.

serves 4

per serving 44.9g fat; 2968kJ

pork chutney burgers

PREPARATION TIME 20 MINUTES ■ COOKING TIME 10 MINUTES

500g minced pork

1 cup (100g) packaged breadcrumbs

1 egg, beaten lightly

1 tablespoon finely chopped fresh flat-leaf parsley

2 tablespoons fruit chutney

2 tablespoons grated cheddar cheese

4 hamburger buns

2 lettuce leaves, shredded

1 medium tomato (190g), sliced thinly

4 canned pineapple rings

1 Combine pork, breadcrumbs, egg and parsley in medium bowl. Using hands, shape mixture into four patties; flatten slightly. Indent centres; spoon combined chutney and cheese into centre of each patty. Shape patties around chutney mixture to enclose mixture; flatten slightly.

2 Cook patties on heated oiled barbecue, uncovered, until browned and cooked through.

3 Split buns in half. Place cut-side down onto barbecue; cook until lightly toasted.

4 Top base of buns with lettuce, tomato, pineapple and patties; top with extra chutney, if desired. Replace top of buns.

serves 4

per serving 14.6g fat; 2096kJ

fish burgers

PREPARATION TIME 15 MINUTES ■ COOKING TIME 20 MINUTES

We used shark (also called flake) in this recipe; it has a
sweet flavour with a soft texture. Other white-fleshed fish can
be substituted.

600g shark fillets, chopped coarsely
1 egg
1/4 teaspoon sweet paprika
1 teaspoon ground cumin
1 teaspoon ground coriander
1/2 teaspoon garlic salt
40cm loaf turkish bread
2 lebanese cucumbers (260g)
3/4 cup (210g) yogurt
1 tablespoon finely chopped fresh mint

1 Blend or process fish, egg, paprika, cumin,
coriander and garlic salt until smooth. Using
hands, shape mixture into four patties.

2 Cook patties on heated oiled barbecue,
uncovered, until browned and cooked through.

3 Cut bread into four pieces; split each in half.
Place cut-side down onto barbecue; cook until
lightly toasted.

4 Using a vegetable peeler, slice cucumbers into
thin strips.

5 Combine remaining ingredients in small bowl.

6 Top bread bases with patties; top with equal
amounts of cucumber and yogurt mixture, then
remaining bread.

serves 4

per serving 6.6g fat; 2193kJ

beef sausages with onion

PREPARATION TIME 5 MINUTES ■ COOKING TIME 10 MINUTES

¼ cup (60ml) barbecue sauce

1 tablespoon worcestershire sauce

1 tablespoon tomato sauce

1 clove garlic, crushed

8 thick beef sausages (920g)

2 medium brown onions (300g),
   sliced thinly

1 Combine sauces and garlic in small bowl.

2 Cook sausages and onion on heated oiled barbecue, uncovered, until browned all over and cooked through, brushing sausages occasionally with sauce mixture during cooking. Serve onion over sausages.

serves 4

per serving   58.6g fat; 2957kJ

gourmet beef burgers

PREPARATION TIME 15 MINUTES ■ COOKING TIME 10 MINUTES

Mesclun is a mixture of assorted young lettuce and other green leaves.

750g minced beef

1 cup (70g) stale breadcrumbs

2 tablespoons finely chopped fresh flat-leaf parsley

2 tablespoons sun-dried tomato paste

125g mozzarella cheese, sliced thinly

½ cup (150g) mayonnaise

4 bread rolls

50g mesclun

1 small red onion (100g), sliced thinly

2 tablespoons drained, sliced sun-dried tomatoes in oil

1 Combine beef, breadcrumbs, parsley and 1½ tablespoons of the paste in large bowl. Using hands, shape mixture into four patties.

2 Cook patties on heated oiled barbecue, uncovered, until browned and cooked through. Top patties with cheese; cook until cheese melts.

3 Combine remaining paste and mayonnaise in small bowl.

4 Split rolls in half. Place cut-side down onto barbecue; cook until lightly toasted.

5 Sandwich patties, mayonnaise mixture, mesclun, onion and sliced tomatoes between bread rolls.

serves 4

per serving 39.2g fat; 3219kJ

lamb burgers with tomato salsa

PREPARATION TIME 30 MINUTES (plus standing and refrigeration time)
COOKING TIME 30 MINUTES

1 medium eggplant (300g)

coarse cooking salt

2 tablespoons olive oil

6 bread rolls

120g rocket

½ cup (40g) flaked parmesan cheese

PATTIES

600g minced lamb

1 medium brown onion (150g), chopped finely

2 cloves garlic, crushed

⅓ cup (50g) drained, chopped sun-dried tomatoes in oil

⅓ cup (50g) seeded black olives, chopped

¾ cup (50g) stale breadcrumbs

2 tablespoons finely chopped fresh basil

1 egg, beaten lightly

TOMATO SALSA

1 large red capsicum (350g)

3 small tomatoes (390g), chopped finely

1 small red onion (100g), chopped finely

1 teaspoon balsamic vinegar

1 teaspoon finely chopped fresh oregano

1 Cut eggplant into 1.5cm slices; place in strainer. Sprinkle with salt; stand 30 minutes.

2 Rinse eggplant under cold running water; drain on absorbent paper. Brush eggplant with oil. Cook eggplant on heated oiled barbecue, uncovered, until browned both sides and tender.

3 Split rolls in half. Place cut-side down onto barbecue; cook until lightly toasted. Fill with eggplant, patties, rocket, cheese and tomato salsa.

patties Combine ingredients in medium bowl; mix well. Using hands, shape mixture into six patties; place on tray. Cover; refrigerate 30 minutes. Cook patties on heated oiled barbecue, uncovered, until browned and cooked through.

tomato salsa Quarter capsicum; remove seeds and membranes. Cook capsicum on heated oiled barbecue, skin-side down, until skin blisters and blackens. Peel away skin, slice capsicum thinly. Combine capsicum with remaining ingredients in medium bowl.

serves 6

per serving 22.4g fat; 2152kJ

burgers with mustard mayonnaise

PREPARATION TIME 20 MINUTES ■ COOKING TIME 15 MINUTES

500g minced beef

½ cup (40g) packaged seasoned stuffing mix

¼ cup (60ml) tomato sauce

¼ cup coarsely chopped fresh flat-leaf parsley

2 large white onions (400g), sliced thinly

4 hamburger buns

8 green oak leaf lettuce leaves

1 large tomato (250g), sliced thinly

1 tablespoon seeded mustard

½ cup (150g) mayonnaise

1 Combine beef, stuffing mix, sauce and parsley in medium bowl. Using hands, shape mixture into four patties.

2 Cook patties on heated oiled barbecue, uncovered, until browned and cooked through.

3 Meanwhile, cook onion on heated oiled barbecue plate until soft and browned.

4 Split buns in half. Place cut-side down onto barbecue; cook until lightly toasted.

5 Top base of buns with lettuce, tomato, patties, combined mustard and mayonnaise, then onion; replace top of buns.

serves 4

per serving   26.6g fat; 2322kJ

chicken burgers with avocado cream

PREPARATION TIME 30 MINUTES ■ COOKING TIME 10 MINUTES

800g minced chicken

**2 rashers lean bacon (140g),
chopped finely**

1/3 cup (25g) grated parmesan cheese

3 green onions, chopped finely

**1 tablespoon finely chopped
fresh thyme**

1 egg, beaten lightly

1/2 cup (50g) packaged breadcrumbs

20cm square focaccia

1 cup (55g) snow pea sprouts

**2 medium tomatoes (260g),
sliced thinly**

1 medium carrot (120g), sliced thinly

AVOCADO CREAM

**1 medium avocado (250g),
chopped coarsely**

**125g packaged cream
cheese, softened**

1 tablespoon lemon juice

1 Combine chicken, bacon, cheese, onion, thyme, egg and breadcrumbs in medium bowl. Using hands, shape mixture into four patties.

2 Cook patties on heated oiled barbecue, uncovered, until browned and cooked through.

3 Cut focaccia into four pieces; split each in half. Place cut-side down onto barbecue; cook until lightly toasted.

4 Top focaccia bases with sprouts, patties, tomato, avocado cream and carrot.

avocado cream Combine ingredients in bowl; mash with a fork until well combined.

serves 4

per serving 45.4g fat; 3473kJ

red onion and balsamic jam

PREPARATION TIME 10 MINUTES
COOKING TIME 20 MINUTES

This jam is suitable to serve with lamb and chicken.

¼ cup (60ml) olive oil
3 medium red onions (510g), sliced thinly
¼ cup (50g) firmly packed brown sugar
⅓ cup (80ml) balsamic vinegar
½ teaspoon dill seeds
¼ cup (60ml) chicken stock

1 Heat oil in medium saucepan; cook onion, stirring until soft and browned lightly.

2 Stir in sugar, vinegar, seeds and stock. Simmer, uncovered, about 20 minutes or until mixture thickens.

makes 1½ cups

per tablespoon 3.1g fat; 198kJ

garlic and hoisin

PREPARATION TIME 10 MINUTES
COOKING TIME 45 MINUTES (plus cooling time)

This Asian-style sauce goes well with pork, beef, lamb or chicken, and is good brushed over kebabs.

1 whole bulb garlic
½ cup (125ml) hoisin sauce
2 tablespoons sweet chilli sauce
1 tablespoon soy sauce
1 tablespoon rice vinegar
1 teaspoon sesame oil
2 tablespoons coarsely chopped fresh coriander

1 Place garlic on a disposable baking tray; cook in covered barbecue, using indirect heat, following manufacturer's instructions, about 45 minutes or until cloves are tender. When cool enough to handle, cut crossways in half; squeeze out garlic.

2 Combine garlic in medium bowl with sauces, vinegar and oil; whisk until smooth. Stir in coriander.

makes 1 cup

per tablespoon 1.2g fat; 147kJ

chilli and coriander

PREPARATION TIME 5 MINUTES
COOKING TIME 15 MINUTES (plus cooling time)

2 large tomatoes (500g), chopped coarsely

¼ cup (60ml) water

⅓ cup (80ml) lime juice

¼ cup (50g) firmly packed brown sugar

1 teaspoon fish sauce

⅓ cup (80ml) sweet chilli sauce

2 tablespoons coarsely chopped fresh coriander

1 Combine tomato, the water, juice, sugar and sauces in medium pan; stir over low heat until sugar dissolves. Bring to a boil; reduce heat. Simmer, uncovered, about 10 minutes or until sauce thickens.

2 Remove from heat; cool. Stir in coriander.

makes 1 cup

per tablespoon 0.3g fat; 127kJ

creamy avocado

PREPARATION TIME 10 MINUTES

1 large avocado (320g)

¼ cup (60g) sour cream

¼ cup (75g) mayonnaise

2 tablespoons olive oil

1 teaspoon Tabasco sauce

1 clove garlic, quartered

¼ cup tightly packed fresh coriander leaves

1 tablespoon lemon juice

1 Blend or process ingredients until smooth.

makes 1½ cups

per tablespoon 7.5g fat; 303kJ

sauces

vegetables

Barbecuing turns vegies from bland to brilliant. It concentrates the flavours and, except for the leafy greens, there's barely a vegetable that can't be barbecued, either alone with a lick of oil, or in one of the delicious dishes in this chapter.

garlic celeriac

PREPARATION TIME 15 MINUTES ■ COOKING TIME 1 HOUR

1 large celeriac (1.5kg)
1 large garlic bulb
2 tablespoons olive oil
⅓ cup chopped fresh
**   flat-leaf parsley**
⅓ cup (95g) yogurt

1 Peel celeriac; cut into 3cm pieces. Combine celeriac and garlic in disposable baking dish; add oil.

2 Cook in covered barbecue, using indirect heat, following manufacturer's instructions, about 1 hour or until celeriac is golden brown and tender, turning occasionally during cooking.

3 Cut garlic in half crossways; squeeze pulp over celeriac. Toss together with parsley.

4 Serve topped with yogurt.

serves 4

per serving 10.8g fat; 809kJ

tomatoes with walnut gremolata

PREPARATION TIME 10 MINUTES ■ COOKING TIME 30 MINUTES

8 medium tomatoes (1.5kg), halved

2 tablespoons balsamic vinegar

WALNUT GREMOLATA

¼ cup (30g) walnuts, chopped finely

2 tablespoons finely grated lemon rind

1 clove garlic, crushed

1 cup finely chopped fresh flat-leaf parsley

1 Place tomatoes, cut-side up, in lightly oiled disposable baking dish; drizzle with vinegar.

2 Cook tomatoes in covered barbecue, using indirect heat, following manufacturer's instructions, about 30 minutes or until soft. Serve with walnut gremolata, and barbecued steak, if desired.

walnut gremolata Combine ingredients in small bowl; mix well.

serves 8

per serving 2.8g fat; 224kJ

potatoes with aïoli

PREPARATION TIME 20 MINUTES ■ COOKING TIME 20 MINUTES

1kg kipfler potatoes

AIOLI
2 egg yolks
2 tablespoons lemon juice
2 cloves garlic, crushed
¾ cup (180ml) olive oil
1 tablespoon hot water

1 Cut potatoes in half lengthways.

2 Cook potato on heated oiled barbecue until tender; serve with aïoli.

aïoli Blend or process egg yolks, juice and garlic until combined. With motor operating, gradually add oil; process until thick. Stir in the water.

serves 4

per serving 44.1g fat; 2346kJ
tip Aïoli can be made a day ahead and refrigerated, covered.

lemon and garlic corn cobs

PREPARATION TIME 15 MINUTES ■ COOKING TIME 15 MINUTES

6 trimmed corn cobs (1.5kg)

2 teaspoons shredded lemon rind

1 tablespoon seeded mustard

2 cloves garlic, crushed

**2 tablespoons coarsely
  chopped chives**

1/3 cup (80ml) lemon juice

1/3 cup (80ml) peanut oil

1 Cook corn on heated oiled barbecue, uncovered, until browned all over.

2 Serve corn drizzled with combined remaining ingredients.

serves 6

per serving 15.1g fat; 1427kJ

tip Recipe can be prepared 2 days ahead and refrigerated, covered.

zucchini with chermoulla dressing

PREPARATION TIME 10 MINUTES ■ COOKING TIME 10 MINUTES

Chermoulla, a seasoning often used as a dry marinade or rub, is an integral part of Moroccan cooking. It consists of onion, garlic, herbs and spices.

8 medium zucchini (1kg)

CHERMOULLA DRESSING

1 small red onion (100g), chopped finely

2 cloves garlic, crushed

½ teaspoon hot paprika

1 teaspoon sweet paprika

1 teaspoon ground cumin

½ cup (125ml) olive oil

2 tablespoons lemon juice

1 cup finely chopped fresh flat-leaf parsley

1 Cut zucchini in half lengthways.

2 Cook zucchini on heated oiled barbecue, uncovered, until browned lightly both sides and just tender.

3 Serve drizzled with chermoulla dressing.

chermoulla dressing Combine ingredients in screw-top jar; shake well.

serves 8

per serving 14.7g fat; 626kJ

garlic and rosemary vegetables

PREPARATION TIME 15 MINUTES
COOKING TIME 1 HOUR 30 MINUTES

Golden nugget pumpkins are small, round pumpkins with orange skin and dark-yellow flesh.

3 golden nugget pumpkins (1.2kg)
1.5kg tiny new potatoes
800g spring onions, trimmed
8 unpeeled cloves garlic
1/3 cup (80ml) olive oil
1/4 cup fresh rosemary leaves

1 Cut pumpkin in quarters; remove and discard seeds. Cut each quarter in half.

2 Combine pumpkin, potatoes, onion, garlic, oil and half of the rosemary in oiled disposable baking dish.

3 Cook in covered barbecue, using indirect heat, following manufacturer's instructions, about 1 1/2 hours or until vegetables are browned and tender, stirring occasionally during cooking.

4 Serve vegetables sprinkled with remaining rosemary.

serves 8

per serving 10.1g fat; 1160kJ

vegetables with haloumi

PREPARATION TIME 30 MINUTES ■ COOKING TIME 35 MINUTES

2 medium yellow zucchini (240g)

2 medium green zucchini (240g)

1 large red capsicum (350g)

1 large yellow capsicum (350g)

4 medium baby eggplants (240g)

4 spring onions (100g)

200g haloumi cheese, sliced thinly

¾ cup (180ml) olive oil

**1 tablespoon caraway
    seeds, toasted**

1 tablespoon grated lemon rind

1 clove garlic, crushed

2 teaspoons ground cumin

**1 tablespoon finely chopped fresh
    lemon thyme**

**2 tablespoons drained, finely
    chopped capers**

1 Thickly slice vegetables lengthways.

2 Cook vegetables and cheese on heated oiled barbecue, uncovered, until browned both sides and tender.

3 Transfer vegetables to large serving platter; drizzle with combined oil, seeds, rind, garlic, cumin, thyme and capers. Serve vegetables topped with cheese.

serves 6

per serving 33.8g fat; 1558kJ

mushrooms with basil butter

PREPARATION TIME 5 MINUTES ■ COOKING TIME 30 MINUTES

100g butter, softened

1 clove garlic, crushed

2 tablespoons seeded mustard

2 tablespoons finely shredded fresh basil

4 flat mushrooms (360g)

1 Combine butter, garlic, mustard and basil in small bowl; top each mushroom with butter mixture.

2 Place mushrooms, butter-side up, in single layer in oiled disposable baking dish.

3 Cook in covered barbecue, using indirect heat, following manufacturer's instructions, about 30 minutes or until tender.

serves 4

per serving 21g fat; 872kJ

pumpkin with walnut dressing

PREPARATION TIME 15 MINUTES ■ COOKING TIME 15 MINUTES

800g pumpkin, sliced thickly

WALNUT DRESSING
½ cup (50g) toasted chopped walnuts
¼ cup (60ml) lemon juice
½ cup (125ml) olive oil
1 tablespoon dijon mustard
2 tablespoons finely chopped fresh chives

1 Cook pumpkin on heated oiled barbecue until browned all over and tender.

2 Serve pumpkin drizzled with walnut dressing.

walnut dressing Combine ingredients in screw-top jar; shake well.

serves 4

per serving 37.9g fat; 1695kJ

roast vegetables with herb and garlic dressing

PREPARATION TIME 30 MINUTES ■ COOKING TIME 30 MINUTES

4 baby eggplants (240g)

4 medium zucchini (480g)

2 large red capsicums (700g)

2 large green capsicums (700g)

400g spring onions, halved

300g swiss brown mushrooms, halved

cooking-oil spray

HERB AND GARLIC DRESSING

1/4 cup finely chopped fresh flat-leaf parsley

2 tablespoons finely chopped fresh mint

2 cloves garlic, crushed

1 fresh red thai chilli, seeded, chopped finely

1/3 cup (80ml) tomato juice

1 teaspoon grated lemon rind

2 tablespoons lemon juice

1½ tablespoons olive oil

1 teaspoon dijon mustard

1 Thickly slice eggplants and zucchini lengthways. Quarter capsicums, remove seeds and membranes.

2 Combine vegetables in oiled disposable baking dish; spray with a little of the cooking-oil spray.

3 Cook in covered barbecue, using indirect heat, following manufacturer's instructions, about 30 minutes or until browned and tender, stirring occasionally during cooking.

4 Peel skin from capsicum. Serve vegetables with herb and garlic dressing.

herb and garlic dressing Combine ingredients in medium jug.

serves 4

per serving 9g fat; 859kJ

potatoes and mushrooms with olives

PREPARATION TIME 10 MINUTES ■ COOKING TIME 45 MINUTES

1/3 cup (80ml) olive oil

6 unpeeled cloves garlic

5 medium potatoes (1kg), unpeeled, quartered

6 baby onions (150g)

350g button mushrooms

1 tablespoon fresh rosemary leaves

1/2 cup (60g) seeded black olives

1/2 cup (55g) drained sun-dried tomatoes in oil, halved

1 tablespoon coarsely chopped fresh flat-leaf parsley

1 Combine oil, garlic, potato, onions, mushrooms and rosemary in oiled disposable baking dish. Cook in covered barbecue, using indirect heat, following manufacturer's instructions, about 45 minutes or until potatoes are browned and tender, stirring occasionally during cooking.

2 Add olives and tomato; mix well. Sprinkle with parsley.

serves 6

per serving 13.4g fat; 1140kJ

char-grilled fruit

PREPARATION TIME 20 MINUTES
COOKING TIME 20 MINUTES

You will need about three passionfruit for this recipe.

½ **medium pineapple (600g)**
2 medium mangoes (860g)
½ **cup (125ml) Malibu**
¼ **cup (60ml) passionfruit pulp**
1 tablespoon brown sugar
300ml thickened cream, whipped
2 tablespoons flaked coconut, toasted

1 Remove and discard top and base from pineapple. Cut pineapple into 1cm-thick slices; cut each slice in half. Cut mangoes down each side of stone; cut a criss-cross pattern into flesh.

2 Combine Malibu, passionfruit pulp and sugar in saucepan. Stir over low heat, without boiling, until sugar dissolves. Simmer, uncovered, 5 minutes. Combine fruit with passionfruit syrup in bowl.

3 Cook fruit, on heated oiled barbecue, until browned both sides and tender, brushing occasionally with some of the syrup during cooking.

4 Drizzle warm fruit with remaining passionfruit syrup. Serve with cream; sprinkle with coconut.

serves 4

per serving 30.1g fat; 2298kJ

figs, honeycomb and cinnamon ice-cream

PREPARATION TIME 15 MINUTES
COOKING TIME 5 MINUTES

Fresh honeycomb is available from health food stores.

6 medium figs (360g)
500g fresh honeycomb
500ml vanilla ice-cream, softened
2 teaspoons ground cinnamon

1 Cut figs in half lengthways; cook on heated oiled barbecue until browned.

2 Cut honeycomb into 2cm strips. Combine ice-cream and cinnamon in medium bowl.

3 Serve hot figs with ice-cream mixture and honeycomb.

serves 4

per serving 7g fat; 2287kJ

pears with ricotta, date and maple filling

PREPARATION TIME 20 MINUTES
COOKING TIME 30 MINUTES

1¼ cups (250g) ricotta cheese
¼ cup (40g) seeded chopped dates
¼ teaspoon ground cinnamon
1 teaspoon sugar
4 medium pears (920g)
½ cup (125ml) maple syrup
¼ cup (60ml) water

1 Combine cheese, dates, cinnamon and sugar in small bowl.

2 Cut pears in half lengthways; using a teaspoon, scoop out seeds. Place a heaped tablespoon of the cheese mixture in hollow of each pear half.

3 Place pears in disposable baking dish; drizzle with combined maple syrup and water.

4 Cover tightly with greased foil; cook in covered barbecue, using indirect heat, following manufacturer's instructions, 30 minutes or until pears are tender. Serve pears drizzled with extra maple syrup, if desired.

serves 8

per serving 3.7g fat; 716kJ

caramelised peaches with spiced yogurt

PREPARATION TIME 25 MINUTES
COOKING TIME 10 MINUTES

6 medium peaches (1.2kg), peeled, halved
¼ cup (50g) firmly packed brown sugar

SPICED YOGURT
¾ cup (210g) yogurt
¼ teaspoon ground cinnamon
¼ teaspoon ground cardamom

1 Cook peaches on heated oiled barbecue grill plate until browned. Sprinkle with sugar; cook, turning, until sugar dissolves and starts to bubble.

2 Serve with spiced yogurt.

spiced yogurt Combine ingredients in small bowl.

serves 4

per serving 2g fat; 685kJ

fruit

salads

No barbie is complete without a favourite salad – tabbouleh, coleslaw, potato or pasta. Or try barbecuing asparagus, green onions, mushrooms or capsicum on an oiled hot plate then adding them to a green salad.

pasta salad

PREPARATION TIME 20 MINUTES (plus cooling time) ■ COOKING TIME 15 MINUTES

We used shell-shaped pasta for this salad, but you can use any small pasta you like – whether it's tubular, like elbow macaroni, or a solid shape, like bow-ties or spirals.

375g shell pasta

6 bacon rashers (420g)

1½ cups (450g) mayonnaise

⅓ cup (90g) seeded mustard

¾ cup (180ml) buttermilk

3 trimmed sticks celery (225g), sliced thinly

1 large red capsicum (350g), chopped finely

½ cup coarsely chopped fresh chives

2 tablespoons finely chopped fresh flat-leaf parsley

1 Cook pasta in large saucepan of boiling water, uncovered, until just tender. Drain; cool.

2 Meanwhile, remove and discard rind from bacon; cut bacon into small pieces. Cook bacon, stirring, in heated medium frying pan until browned and crisp; drain on absorbent paper.

3 Whisk mayonnaise, mustard and buttermilk in large bowl.

4 Add pasta, bacon and remaining ingredients to bowl; toss gently to combine.

serves 6

per serving 32.1g fat; 2684kJ

tips Rinse cooked, drained pasta under warm running water, then under cold running water, to prepare salad more quickly.

Blend about 2 teaspoons of your favourite curry powder with the mayonnaise mixture for another flavour variation.

herb coleslaw with lemon dressing

PREPARATION TIME 25 MINUTES

This is a perfect coleslaw for people who don't care for creamy salad dressings.

1 medium white cabbage (1.5kg), shredded finely

15 green onions, chopped finely

1 cup coarsely chopped fresh mint

1/2 cup coarsely chopped fresh flat-leaf parsley

1/4 cup coarsely chopped fresh coriander

LEMON DRESSING

1/4 cup (60ml) lemon juice

1 tablespoon dijon mustard

1/2 cup (125ml) peanut oil

1 Combine cabbage in large bowl with onion and herbs.

2 Pour lemon dressing over salad; toss to combine.

lemon dressing Combine ingredients in screw-top jar; shake well.

serves 8

per serving   14.6g fat; 708kJ

three-bean salad

PREPARATION TIME 35 MINUTES

300g can butter beans, rinsed, drained

300g can red kidney beans, rinsed, drained

500g packet frozen broad beans, thawed, peeled

**1 medium tomato (190g), peeled, seeded,
   chopped coarsely**

1 small red onion (100g), chopped coarsely

¼ cup coarsely chopped fresh flat-leaf parsley

DRESSING

¼ cup (60ml) olive oil

¼ cup (60ml) lemon juice

1 clove garlic, crushed

½ teaspoon sugar

½ teaspoon cracked black pepper

1 Combine beans with tomato, onion and parsley in large bowl.

2 Add dressing; mix well.

dressing Combine ingredients in screw-top jar; shake well.

serves 6

per serving 9.6g fat; 682kJ

german hot potato salad

PREPARATION TIME 10 MINUTES (plus cooling time) ■ COOKING TIME 20 MINUTES

4 eggs

**4 bacon rashers (280g),
   chopped coarsely**

750g tiny new potatoes

2 pickled gherkins, chopped finely

**1 tablespoon finely chopped fresh
   flat-leaf parsley**

2/3 cup (200g) mayonnaise

1/3 cup (80g) sour cream

2 teaspoons lemon juice

1 Cover eggs with water in medium saucepan. Bring to a boil; reduce
   heat. Simmer, uncovered, 10 minutes; drain. Cool eggs under cold water;
   shell and halve.

2 Meanwhile, cook bacon, stirring, in heated medium frying pan until browned
   and crisp; drain on absorbent paper.

3 Boil, steam or microwave potatoes until tender; drain and halve.

4 Combine remaining ingredients in large saucepan; stir over low heat until just
   hot. Place mayonnaise mixture in large bowl with potato, bacon and egg; toss
   gently to combine.

serves 4

per serving 35.6g fat; 2414kJ

tip Bacon can be cooked and eggs hard-boiled a few hours beforehand. The potato halves and
mayonnaise dressing should be hot just before serving time.

baby rocket and parmesan salad

PREPARATION TIME 20 MINUTES ■ COOKING TIME 3 MINUTES

60g parmesan cheese

200g baby rocket leaves

**80g semi-dried tomatoes,
  halved lengthways**

¼ cup (40g) pine nuts, toasted

¼ cup (60ml) balsamic vinegar

¼ cup (60ml) olive oil

1 Using vegetable peeler, shave cheese into long, wide pieces.

2 Combine rocket with tomato and pine nuts in large bowl; add cheese. Drizzle with combined vinegar and oil; toss gently.

serves 8

per serving 13.7g fat; 673kJ

tip Baby spinach leaves can be substituted for the rocket in this recipe.

mesclun with pine nuts in lime vinaigrette

PREPARATION TIME 15 MINUTES (plus standing time)

Mesclun is a mixture of assorted young lettuce
and other green leaves.

4 green onions
400g mesclun
¼ cup (40g) pine nuts, toasted

LIME VINAIGRETTE
¼ cup (60ml) lime juice
¼ cup (60ml) peanut oil
2 cloves garlic, crushed
1 teaspoon sugar

1 Cut onions into 10cm lengths; slice thinly
lengthways. Place onion in bowl of iced water;
stand about 10 minutes or until onion curls.

2 Place drained onion in large bowl with mesclun
and pine nuts; toss gently with lime vinaigrette.

lime vinaigrette Combine ingredients in
screw-top jar; shake well.

serves 8

per serving 10.5g fat; 447kJ
tip Trimmed onions can be placed in a small bowl of water
and refrigerated, covered, overnight.

sliced tomato, basil and red onion salad

PREPARATION TIME 15 MINUTES

**4 large egg tomatoes (360g),
sliced thinly**

**1 small red onion (100g),
sliced thinly**

**2 tablespoons small fresh
basil leaves**

cracked black pepper

1/4 teaspoon sugar

2 teaspoons balsamic vinegar

2 teaspoons olive oil

1 Alternate layers of tomato, onion and basil on serving plate; sprinkle with pepper and sugar.

2 Drizzle with combined vinegar and oil.

serves 4

per serving 2.4g fat; 170kJ

tip This salad is best assembled up to 3 hours ahead and refrigerated, covered, so that the delightful piquancy of the flavours can blend.

tabbouleh

PREPARATION TIME 40 MINUTES (plus refrigeration time)

Tabbouleh is a delicious Middle Eastern salad, and one of the most nutritionally sound dishes we can think of. It contains plenty of fibre as well as healthy proportions of vitamin C.

3 medium tomatoes (570g)

1/2 cup (80g) burghul

5 cups tightly packed fresh flat-leaf parsley, chopped coarsely

1 medium red onion (170g), chopped finely

1 cup tightly packed fresh mint, chopped coarsely

1/4 cup (60ml) lemon juice

1/4 cup (60ml) olive oil

1 Chop tomatoes finely, retaining as much of the juice as possible. Place tomato and juice on top of burghul in small bowl. Cover; refrigerate at least 2 hours or until burghul is soft.

2 Combine parsley, onion and mint in large bowl with burghul mixture and remaining ingredients; toss gently to combine.

serves 4

per serving 14.9g fat; 862kJ

barbecued potatoes in foil

Pierce four large potatoes (1.2kg) with fork; wrap individually in foil. Cook potatoes in covered barbecue using indirect heat, following manufacturer's instructions, about 1 hour or until cooked through. Unwrap potatoes; cut a deep cross in potato. Gently squeeze with tongs to open; top with one of the following toppings.

serves 4

per serving 0.3g fat; 819kJ

avocado and tomato salsa

PREPARATION TIME 15 MINUTES

1 medium avocado (250g), chopped finely

2 medium tomatoes (380g), chopped finely

1 tablespoon coarsely chopped fresh flat-leaf parsley

1 Combine ingredients in small bowl. Serve hot potatoes topped with avocado and tomato salsa.

serves 4

per serving 10g fat; 438kJ

pesto butter

PREPARATION TIME 10 MINUTES (plus refrigeration time)
COOKING TIME 3 MINUTES

125g butter, softened

¼ cup (40g) pine nuts, toasted, chopped coarsely

¼ cup (20g) finely grated parmesan cheese

¼ cup (65g) bottled basil pesto

½ teaspoon cracked black pepper

1 Beat butter in small bowl with electric mixer until light and creamy; stir in remaining ingredients. Cover tightly; refrigerate until firm.

2 Serve hot potatoes topped with pesto butter.

serves 4

per serving 40.7g fat; 1605kJ

bacon and cheese

PREPARATION TIME 10 MINUTES
COOKING TIME 10 MINUTES

3 rashers bacon (210g), sliced thinly
1 cup (125g) grated cheddar cheese
2 tablespoons finely chopped fresh chives

1 Cook bacon, stirring, in heated medium frying pan until browned and crisp; drain on absorbent paper.

2 Sprinkle cheese over hot potatoes; top with bacon and chives.

serves 4

per serving 15.2g fat; 887kJ

sour cream with sweet chilli sauce

PREPARATION TIME 5 MINUTES

3/4 cup (200g) sour cream
2 tablespoons sweet chilli sauce
2 tablespoons finely chopped fresh coriander

1 Combine ingredients in medium bowl; spoon onto hot potatoes.

serves 4

per serving 20.1g fat; 829kJ

potatoes

glossary

allspice also known as pimento or jamaican pepper; available whole or ground.

artichoke hearts tender centre of the globe artichoke; purchased in brine canned or in jars.

bacon rashers slices of bacon; made from pork side, cured and smoked.

balmain bugs crustacean; a type of crayfish.

barbecue sauce a spicy, tomato-based sauce used to marinate, baste or as an accompaniment.

basil an aromatic herb; there are many types, but the most commonly used is sweet basil.

purple also known as opal basil, has an intense aroma and a longer shelf life than sweet basil.

thai also known as bai kaprow or holy basil; has small crinkly leaves, purple stems and a strong, slightly bitter flavour.

bay leaves aromatic leaves from the bay tree; use fresh or dried.

bean sprouts also known as bean shoots; tender new growths of assorted beans and seeds germinated for consumption as sprouts.

beans

butter also known as lima beans, sold both dried and canned. A large beige bean having a mealy texture and mild taste.

broad also known as fava beans; available fresh, canned and frozen. Best peeled twice (discarding both the outer long green pod and the sandy-green tough inner shell).

green sometimes called french beans.

red kidney have a floury texture and fairly sweet flavour; colour can vary from pink to maroon.

salted black soybeans which have been salted and fermented; chop or crush lightly before using.

beef

rib eye (scotch fillet) the section of eye muscle which runs through the forequarter.

rump boneless tender cut.

T-bone steak with the bone in and fillet eye attached.

minced also known as ground beef.

beetroot also known as beets or red beets; firm, round sweet root vegetable.

black mussels must be tightly closed when bought, indicating they are alive. Before cooking, scrub the shells with a strong brush to remove the "beards". Discard any shells that do not open after cooking.

black mustard seeds also known as brown mustard seeds.

blue swimmer crabs also known as sand crabs, atlantic blue crabs.

blue-eye also known as deep-sea trevalla or trevally and blue-eye cod; thick, moist white-fleshed fish.

bread

ciabatta meaning "slipper" in Italian, the traditional shape of this popular crisp-crusted white bread.

foccacia a flat Italian-style bread.

lavash flat, unleavened bread of Mediterranean origin.

naan leavened bread that is baked pressed against the inside wall of a heated tandoor or clay oven.

pitta (lebanese bread) also spelled pita; wheat-flour pocket bread sold in large, flat pieces, separating easily into two paper-thin rounds. Also pocket pitta.

turkish (pide) comes in long (about 40cm) flat loaves as well as individual rounds; made from wheat flour and sprinkled with sesame or black onion seeds.

breadcrumbs

packaged fine-textured, crunchy, purchased, white breadcrumbs.

stale 1- or 2-day-old bread made into crumbs by grating, blending or processing.

burghul also known as bulghur wheat; hulled steamed wheat kernels that, once dried, are crushed into various size grains.

butter use salted or unsalted ("sweet") butter; 125g is equal to one stick of butter.

buttermilk fresh low-fat milk cultured to give a slightly sour, tangy taste; low-fat yogurt or milk can be substituted.

cabbage

savoy large, heavy head with crinkled dark-green outer leaves; a fairly mild tasting cabbage.

white the common round cabbage.

cajun seasoning packaged blend of assorted herbs and spices; can include paprika, basil, onion, fennel, thyme, cayenne and tarragon.

capers the grey-green buds of a warm climate shrub sold either dried and salted or pickled in vinegar brine.

capsicum also known as pepper or bell pepper; seeds and membranes should be discarded before use.

caraway seeds a member of the parsley family; available in seed or ground form.

cardamom available in pod, seed or ground form; has a distinctive, aromatic flavour.

cashews slightly sweet nuts; we used unsalted roasted cashews.

celeriac tuberous root with brown skin, white flesh and a celery-like flavour.

cheese

bocconcini small rounds of fresh "baby" mozzarella; a delicate, semi-soft, white cheese. Spoils rapidly; keep refrigerated, in brine, for 1 or 2 days only.

cheddar the most common cow milk "tasty" cheese; should be aged and hard.

fetta a crumbly textured goat- or sheep-milk cheese with a sharp, salty taste.

haloumi a firm, cream-coloured sheep milk cheese matured in brine; can be grilled or fried, briefly, without breaking down.

mozzarella a semi-soft cheese with a delicate, fresh taste; has a low melting point and stringy texture when hot.

packaged cream commonly known as "Philadelphia" or "Philly", a soft milk cheese having no less than 33% butterfat.

parmesan a sharp-tasting, dry, hard cheese, made from skim or part-skim milk and aged for at least a year.

pizza a commercial blend of varying proportions of processed grated mozzarella, cheddar and parmesan.

ricotta a sweet, fairly moist, fresh curd cheese having a low fat content.

smoked cheddar a hard cheddar cheese which has been placed, un-cut, in a smoke room. There is also artificially smoked cheese where flavour is added to the milk before the cheese is made.

chicken

breast fillets breast halved, skinned and boned.

drumstick leg with skin intact.

tenderloins the strip of meat lying just under the breast.

thigh cutlets thigh with skin and centre bone intact; sometimes known as a chicken chop.

thigh fillets thigh skinned and boned.

wings have skin and bones with a little meat.

chickpeas also called garbanzos, hummus or channa; an irregularly round, sandy-coloured legume.

chillies available in many types and sizes, both fresh and dried. The smaller the chilli, the hotter it is. Wear rubber gloves when handling chillies, as they can burn your skin. Removing seeds and membranes lessens the heat level.

chilli

flakes crushed dried chillies.

powder the Asian variety is the hottest, made from ground chillies; it can be used as a substitute for fresh chillies in the proportion of 1/2 teaspoon ground chilli powder to 1 medium chopped fresh chilli.

sweet chilli sauce mild, Thai sauce made from red chillies, sugar, garlic and vinegar.

thai small, medium hot, and bright-red to dark-green in colour.

chinese broccoli also known as gai lum and gai larn; leaves and stem are used.

chives related to the onion and leek, with subtle onion flavour.

chorizo a sausage of Spanish origin, made of coarsely ground pork and highly seasoned with garlic and chillies.

choy sum also known as flowering bok choy or flowering white cabbage. The whole plant can be used.

cinnamon dried inner bark of the shoots of the cinnamon tree; available in stick or ground form.

cloves dried flower buds of a tropical tree; can be used whole or in ground form.

coconut

flaked dried, flaked coconut flesh.

shredded thin strips of dried coconut.

cooking oil spray we used a cholesterol-free cooking spray made from canola oil.

coriander

dried a fragrant herb; coriander seeds and ground coriander must never be used to replace fresh coriander or vice versa. The tastes are completely different.

fresh also known as cilantro or chinese parsley; bright-green-leafed herb with a pungent flavour.

corn kernels sometimes called niblets; available canned and frozen.

cornflour also known as cornstarch; used as a thickening agent in cooking.

couscous a fine, grain-like cereal product, made from semolina.

cream we used fresh cream in this book, unless otherwise stated. Also known as pure cream and pouring cream; has no additives unlike commercially thickened cream. Minimum fat content 35%.

sour a thick commercially-cultured soured cream. Minimum fat content 35%.

thickened a whipping cream containing a thickener. Minimum fat content 35%.

cucumber

lebanese small, slender and thin-skinned with juicy flesh and tiny seeds.

telegraph long and slender, also known as burpless or european cucumber.

cumin available both ground and as whole seeds; cumin has a warm, earthy, rather strong flavour.

curly endive also known as frisee; a curly-leafed green vegetable, mainly used in salads.

curry powder a blend of ground spices; choose mild or hot to suit your taste and the recipe.

eggplant also known as aubergine. Depending on their age, they may have to be sliced and salted to reduce their bitterness. Rinse and dry well before use.

baby also known as japanese eggplant, these are small and slender. They don't need to be salted before use.

fish sauce also called nam pla or nuoc nam; made from pulverised salted fermented fish, mostly anchovies. Has a pungent smell and strong taste; use sparingly.

five-spice powder a fragrant mixture of ground cinnamon, cloves, star anise, sichuan pepper and fennel seeds.

flat-leaf parsley also known as continental parsley or italian parsley.

flour

plain an all-purpose wheat flour.

self-raising plain flour sifted with baking powder in the proportion of 1 cup flour to 2 teaspoons baking powder.

food colouring available in liquid, powdered and concentrated paste forms.

garam masala a blend of spices based on varying proportions of cardamom, cinnamon, cloves, coriander, fennel and cumin, roasted and ground together. Black pepper and chilli can be added for a hotter version.

gherkins also known as cornichon; young, dark-green cucumbers grown for pickling.

ginger also known as green or root ginger; the thick gnarled root of a tropical plant.

hoisin sauce a thick, sweet and spicy Chinese paste made from salted fermented soy beans, onions and garlic.

honeycomb the structure made of beeswax that houses the honey; this edible chewy comb, saturated with honey, is available in health food stores and some supermarkets.

kaffir lime leaves aromatic leaves of a small citrus tree bearing a wrinkled-skinned yellow-green fruit; can be used fresh or dried.

kecap manis also called ketjap manis; an Indonesian sweet, thick soy sauce which has sugar and spices added.

kumara orange-fleshed sweet potato often confused with yam.

lamb

chump chops cut from just above the hind legs to the mid-loin section; can be used whole, for roasting, or cut into chops.

cutlets small, tender rib chop; all fat and gristle from end of bone is removed.

eye of loin a cut derived from a row of loin chops. Once the bone and fat are removed, the larger portion is referred to as the eye of the loin.

fillets tenderloin; the smaller piece of meat from a row of loin chops or cutlets.

forequarter chops from the shoulder end of the sheep. They tend to be fatty so are ideal for braising and casseroles. Leaner forequarter chops can be grilled.

leg cut from the hindquarter.

loin row of eight ribs from the tender mid-section.

shoulder, boned boneless section of the forequarter, rolled and secured with string or netting.

diced cubed lean meat.

minced ground lamb.

lemon grass a tall, clumping, lemon-smelling and tasting, sharp edged grass; use only the white lower part of each stem.

lemon pepper seasoning a blend of black pepper, lemon, herbs and spices.

lemon thyme a variety of thyme with a lemony fragrance.

lentils dried pulses often identified by and named by their colour; also known as dhal.

lettuce

oak leaf also known as feville de chene. Available in both red and green leaf.

butter a round, dark green lettuce with soft leaves.

lobster in Australia, this crustacean is correctly known as rock lobster; a crayfish.

Malibu coconut-flavoured rum.

maple syrup a thin syrup distilled from the sap of the maple tree. Maple-flavoured syrup or pancake syrup is not an adequate substitute.

mesclun salad mix or gourmet salad mix; a mixture of assorted young lettuce and other green leaves.

moroccan seasoning packed blend of assorted herbs and spices.

mushrooms

button small, cultivated white mushrooms having a delicate, subtle flavour.

flat a rich earthy flavour; sometimes misnamed field mushrooms.

oyster grey-white fan-shaped mushrooms.

swiss brown light to dark brown mushrooms with full-bodied flavour. Button or cup mushrooms can be substituted.

mustard

powder finely ground white (yellow) mustard seeds.

dijon a pale brown, distinctively flavoured fairly mild French mustard.

french plain mild mustard.

seeded also known as wholegrain. A French-style coarse-grain mustard made from crushed mustard seeds and Dijon-style French mustard.

oil

olive mono-unsaturated; made from the pressing of tree-ripened olives. Extra virgin and virgin are the best, obtained from the first pressings of the olive, while extra light or light refers to the taste, not fat levels.

peanut pressed from ground peanuts; most commonly used in Asian cooking because of its high smoke point.

sesame made from roasted, crushed, white sesame seeds; a flavouring rather than a cooking medium.

vegetable any of a number of oils sourced from plants rather than animal fats.

onion

green also known as scallion or (incorrectly) shallot; an immature onion picked before the bulb has formed, having a long, bright-green edible stalk.

red also known as spanish, red spanish or bermuda onion; a sweet-flavoured, large, purple-red onion.

spring has a crisp, narrow green-leafed top and a fairly large sweet white bulb.

oyster sauce a rich brown sauce made from oysters and their brine; cooked with salt and soy sauce, thickened with starch.

packet taco seasoning a packaged seasoning mix meant to duplicate the Mexican sauce made of oregano, cumin, chillies and various other spices.

paprika ground dried red capsicum (bell pepper); available sweet or hot.

pecans golden-brown, buttery, rich nuts.

peppercorns available in black, white, red or green.

pesto a paste made from fresh basil, oil, garlic, pine nuts and parmesan.

pine nuts also known as pignoli; small, cream-coloured kernels obtained from the cones of different varieties of pine trees.

pistachios pale green, delicately flavoured nut inside hard off-white shells. To peel, soak shelled nuts in boiling water about 5 minutes; drain, then pat dry.

pizza bases commercially packaged, pre-cooked, wheat-flour round bases.

plum sauce a thick, sweet and sour dipping sauce made from plums, vinegar, sugar, chillies and spices.

pork

butterfly steaks skinless, boneless mid-loin chop, split in half and flattened.

fillet skinless, boneless eye-fillet cut from the loin.

loin from pork middle.

neck sometimes called pork scotch, boneless cut from the foreloin.

spare ribs, american-style well-trimmed mid loin ribs.

potato

unwashed

washed

kipfler finger-length, light-brown skinned, nutty flavoured potato.

tiny new also known as chats. Not a particular type of potato but simply an early harvest.

prawns also known as shrimp.

pumpkin also called squash. The various types are interchangeable.

quails small, delicate flavoured, domestically grown game birds ranging in weight from 250g to 300g.

radish a peppery root vegetable related to the mustard plant. The small round red variety is the mildest, it is crisp and juicy and usually eaten raw in salads.

rice

long grain elongated grain, remains separate when cooked; most popular steaming rice in Asia.

rocket also known as arugula, rugula and rucola; a peppery-tasting green leaf. Also baby rocket.

sambal oelek (also ulek or olek) a salty paste made from ground chillies.

seasoned pepper a packaged preparation of combined black pepper, red capsicum (bell pepper), paprika and garlic.

sesame seeds black and white are the most common of these tiny oval seeds; a good source of calcium.

snow peas also called mange tout ('eat all').

soy sauce made from fermented soy beans; several variations are available.

spatchcock a small chicken (poussin), no more than 6 weeks old, weighing a maximum 500g. Also a cooking technique where a small chicken is split open, then flattened and grilled.

squid hoods convenient cleaned squid.

star anise a dried star-shaped pod; seeds have an astringent aniseed flavour.

sun-dried tomatoes dried tomatoes sometimes bottled in oil.

tabasco sauce brand name of an extremely fiery sauce made from vinegar, hot red peppers and salt.

tahini a rich, buttery paste made from crushed sesame seeds.

tamarind sauce if unavailable, soak about 30g dried tamarind in a cup of hot water. Stand 10 minutes and squeeze pulp as dry as possible; use the flavoured water.

tandoori paste Indian blend of hot and fragrant spices including turmeric, paprika, chilli powder, saffron, cardamom and garam masala.

teriyaki marinade a blend of soy sauce, wine, vinegar and spices.

tomato

paste triple-concentrated tomato puree used to flavour soups, stews, sauces and casseroles.

sauce also known as ketchup or catsup; a flavoured condiment made from tomatoes, vinegar and spices.

egg also known as plum or roma, smallish, oval-shaped tomatoes.

cherry also known as tiny tim or tom thumb tomatoes; small and round.

tortillas unleavened, round bread; available frozen, fresh or vacuum-packed.

turmeric a member of the ginger family, its root is dried and ground; intensely pungent in taste but not hot.

veal

cutlets choice chop from the mid-loin (back) area.

steaks schnitzel.

vinegar

balsamic authentic only from the province of Modena, Italy; made from a regional wine of white trebbiano grapes specially processed then aged in antique wooden casks to give the exquisite pungent flavour.

malt made from fermented malt and beech shavings.

red wine based on fermented red wine.

rice based on fermented rice.

white made from spirit of cane sugar.

white wine based on fermented white wine.

watercress small, crisp, deep-green, rounded leaves having a slightly bitter, peppery flavour.

wine we use good-quality dry white and red wines in our recipes.

green ginger beverage 14% alcohol by volume, has the taste of fresh ginger. In cooking, substitute dry (white) vermouth if you prefer.

worcestershire sauce a thin, dark-brown spicy sauce.

zucchini also known as courgette; green yellow or grey members of the squash family having edible flowers.

index

aïoli open sandwiches,
  steak and 158

aïoli, potatoes with 212

american-style pork
  spare ribs 14

artichokes, cutlets with 68

asian-style fish 50

avocado and
  tomato salsa 238

avocado cream, chicken
  burgers with 205

avocado mash, basil
  prawns with 20

avocado, creamy
  (sauce) 207

baba ghanoush, lamb
  kebabs with 25

baby rocket and
  parmesan salad 233

bacon and cheese 239

bacon butter, oysters in 12

balmain bugs
  with oregano 54

balsamic and
  ginger beef 154

balsamic beef with
  grilled eggplant 165

balsamic garlic octopus 28

balsamic jam, red
  onion and 206

balsamic vinegar
  marinade 170

barbecued potatoes
  in foil 238

barramundi with yogurt
  and ginger 40

basil prawns with
  avocado mash 20

beef and onion kebabs 145

beef burgers, gourmet 201

beef fajitas 153

beef kebabs, teriyaki 152

beef ribs, sweet chilli 142

beef sausages
  with onion 200

beef skewers on
  lettuce cups 136

beef spareribs 157

beef, balsamic
  and ginger 154

beef, balsamic, with
  grilled eggplant 165

beef, peppered 164

beef, port-smoked 160

beef, tandoori, with
  grilled limes 149

beetroot tzatziki 36

black bean and chilli
  prawn kebabs 34

blackened fish with burnt
  lemon butter 53

bombay-spiced
  chicken skewers 92

bread, mozzarella turkish,
  olive tapenade and 72

bread, pesto 73

bruschetta 73

burgers with
  mustard mayonnaise 204

burgers, chicken, with
  avocado cream 205

burgers, fish 198

burgers, gourmet beef 201

burgers, lamb, with
  tomato salsa 202

burgers, mexican 192

burgers, pork chutney 197

burghul, lamb
  and, sausages 196

butter, bacon, oysters in 12

butter, basil,
  mushrooms with 219

butter, burnt lemon,
  blackened fish with 53

butter, garlic,
  mussels with 22

butter, pesto 238

butter, tomato and chilli,
  fish steaks with 57

cajun seafood kebabs
  with avocado salsa 64

capers, haloumi with 17

capsicum pesto and
  mashed kumara,
  rib steaks with 162

caramelised peaches
  with spiced yogurt 225

celeriac, garlic 210

char-grilled fruit 224

cheese, bacon and 239

chermoulla dressing,
  zucchini with 215

chermoulla, lamb, with
  chickpea salad 117

chicken breast, chutney,
  with kashmiri pilaf 77

chicken burgers with
  avocado cream 205

chicken cutlets, sesame 89

chicken drumsticks,
  sweet chilli 76

chicken kebabs with
  coriander pesto 33

chicken kebabs, herbed,
  with roasted pecans 88

chicken on lemon
  grass skewers 94

chicken satay 80

chicken skewers,
  bombay-spiced 92

chicken sticks, glazed 30

chicken wings,
  marinated 26

chicken with lentil salsa ... 100

chicken, lemon
  rosemary, with
  couscous seasoning 96

chicken, mediterranean 93

chicken, mustard
  rosemary 81

chicken, portuguese 90

chicken, thyme, with
  grilled citrus 85

chickpea salad, lamb
  chermoulla with 117

chilli and
  coriander (sauce) 207

chilli and honey lamb 104

chilli lime sauce, prawn
  kebabs with 29

chilli plum crabs 58

chilli prawn kebabs,
  black bean and 34

chinese marinated pork ... 176

chops, lamb, with sun-
  dried tomato pesto 126

chops, veal, with
  chickpea and
  tomato salad 144

chorizo pizza 132

chutney chicken breast
  with kashmiri pilaf 77

chutney, mango, indian
  pork kebabs with 178

coconut prawns with
  turmeric coriander
  mayonnaise 45

coleslaw, herb, with
  lemon dressing 229

coriander, chilli
  and (sauce) 207

corn cobs, lemon
  and garlic 214

couscous seasoning,
  lemon rosemary
  chicken with 96

crabs, chilli plum 58

creamy avocado
  (sauce) 207

cumin fish cutlets
  with coriander
  chilli sauce 66

curried cutlets,
  grilled, with tomato
  chickpea salad 129

cutlets with artichokes 68

cutlets, cumin fish,
  with coriander
  chilli sauce 66

cutlets, fish, thai-style 52

cutlets, grilled
  curried, with tomato
  chickpea salad 129

cutlets, lemon pepper,
  with green pea puree ... 112

cutlets, lime-marinated,
  with tomato and
  onion salsa 46

cutlets, moroccan-
  style lamb 16

cutlets, sesame chicken 89

cutlets, spicy veal 150

cutlets, tandoori lamb,
  with cucumber salad 125

cutlets, veal, in
  maple marinade 156

damper, spinach
  and fetta 72

date and maple filling,
  pears with ricotta, ... 225

devilled squid with
  lime vinaigrette 13

dip, eggplant parsley 36

dip, sweet chilli 37

dressing, chermoulla,
  zucchini with 215

dressing, herb and
  garlic, roast
  vegetables with 222

dressing, lemon, herb
  coleslaw with 229

dressing, walnut,
  pumpkin with 220

drumsticks, sweet
  chilli chicken 76

drumsticks, tandoori 78

eggplant parsley dip 36

eggplant, grilled,
  balsamic beef with 165

fajitas beef 153

fetta, spinach
  and, damper 72

figs, honeycomb and
  cinnamon ice-cream 224

fish burgers 198

fish cutlets, cumin,
  with coriander
  chilli sauce 66

fish cutlets, thai-style 52

fish kebabs, pesto 56

fish parcels, soy
  and chilli 60

fish steaks with tomato
  and chilli butter 57

fish, asian-style 50

fish, blackened, with
  burnt lemon butter 53

fish, sweet chilli lime 70

fruit, char-grilled 224

garlic and hoisin
  (sauce) 206

garlic and rosemary
  smoked lamb 122

garlic and rosemary
  vegetables 216

garlic celeriac 210

garlic prawns 32

gemfish kebabs 41

german hot
  potato salad 232

ginger, barramundi
  with yogurt and 40

glaze, honey, spiced
  pork skewers with 174

glaze, lamb with plum 116

glazed chicken sticks 30

gourmet beef burgers 201

greek lamb with lemon
  and potatoes 114

gremolata, walnut,
  tomatoes with 211

gremolata-crumbed
  roast leg of lamb 105

grilled curried cutlets
  with tomato
  chickpea salad 129

grilled lime and
    pepper ocean trout........65
haloumi kebabs,
    lamb and 124
haloumi with capers 17
haloumi, vegetables with..218
ham, orange-glazed........188
herb coleslaw with
    lemon dressing............229
herbed chicken kebabs
    with roasted pecans.......88
herbed lamb steaks 128
herbs, lobster with
    lime and.........................44
hoisin pork kebabs...........184
hoisin, garlic
    and (sauce) 206
honey mustard
    glazed ribs...................183
honey soy marinade.........171
honeycomb and cinnamon
    ice-cream, figs,............224
hot dogs, sausage and
    caramelised onion........193
hummus and tabbouleh,
    lamb kofta with 110
ice-cream, figs, honeycomb
    and cinnamon...............224
indian pork kebabs with
    mango chutney............178
indian spatchcock
    with green chilli
    and coriander...............82
jam, red onion
    and balsamic................206
jam, tomato, pepper
    lamb steaks with...........118
kebabs with mint and
    pistachio pesto............121
kebabs, beef and onion ...145
kebabs, black bean
    and chilli prawn 34
kebabs, cajun seafood,
    with avocado salsa.........64
kebabs, chicken, with
    coriander pesto 33
kebabs, gemfish...............41
kebabs, herbed chicken,
    with roasted pecans.......88
kebabs, hoisin pork..........184
kebabs, indian pork,
    with mango chutney 178
kebabs, lamb
    and haloumi..................124
kebabs, lamb, with
    baba ghanoush 25
kebabs, pesto fish.............56
kebabs, prawn, with
    chilli lime sauce.............29
kebabs, spicy pork...........180
kebabs, teriyaki beef........152
kofta, lamb, with hummus
    and tabbouleh 110
kumara, mashed, rib
    steaks with capsicum
    pesto and 162
lamb and
    burghul sausages.........196

lamb and
    haloumi kebabs 124
lamb burgers with
    tomato salsa 202
lamb chermoulla with
    chickpea salad.............117
lamb chops with sun-dried
    tomato pesto................126
lamb cutlets,
    moroccan-style...............16
lamb cutlets, tandoori,
    with cucumber salad....125
lamb in fruity
    chutney marinade.........108
lamb kebabs with
    baba ghanoush 25
lamb kofta with hummus
    and tabbouleh 110
lamb souvlakia 106
lamb steaks, herbed 128
lamb steaks, pepper,
    with tomato jam 118
lamb with plum glaze 116
lamb, chilli and honey 104
lamb, garlic and
    rosemary smoked.........122
lamb, greek, with lemon
    and potatoes 114
lamb, roast leg of, with garlic
    and rosemary 120
lamb, minted butterflied
    leg of.............................130
lamb, roast leg of,
    gremolata-crumbed......105
lamb, sesame...................113
lamb, tandoori, naan 109
lemon and garlic
    corn cobs 214
lemon pepper
    cutlets with green
    pea puree.....................112
lemon rosemary
    chicken with
    couscous seasoning 96
lentil salsa,
    chicken with..................100
lime and
    coriander octopus 21
lime and mustard,
    turkey with 86
lime fish, sweet chilli 70
lime-marinated cutlets
    with tomato and
    onion salsa 46
lobster with lime
    and herbs 44
mandarin salad,
    pork and 186
marinade, balsamic
    vinegar.........................170
marinade, fruity chutney,
    lamb in.........................108
marinade, honey soy........171
marinade, maple, veal
    cutlets in 156
marinade, red wine 170
marinade, yogurt.............171
marinated chicken wings ...26

marjoram and
    orange turkey 97
mayonnaise, mustard,
    burgers with.................204
mayonnaise, turmeric
    coriander, coconut
    prawns with 45
mediterranean chicken 93
mediterranean steak
    towers 166
mesclun with pine nuts
    in lime vinaigrette 234
mexican burgers 192
middle eastern spicy
    roasted spatchcocks......98
minted butterflied
    leg of lamb 130
moroccan-style
    lamb cutlets 16
mozzarella turkish bread,
    olive tapenade and 72
mushrooms with
    basil butter...................219
mushrooms with olives,
    potatoes and 223
mussels with
    garlic butter 22
mustard mayonnaise,
    burgers with.................204
mustard rosemary
    chicken 81
mustard T-bone with
    jacket potato 148
naan, tandoori lamb 109
nutty rice snapper 61
octopus, balsamic garlic....28
octopus, lime
    and coriander 21
olive paste,
    swordfish with................62
olive salsa, tuna with 42
olive tapenade
    and mozzarella
    turkish bread 72
olives, potatoes and
    mushrooms with 223
onion kebabs,
    beef and 145
orange-glazed ham..........188
orange turkey,
    marjoram and 97
oregano, balmain
    bugs with 54
oysters in bacon butter 12
parmesan salad, baby
    rocket and 233
pasta salad......................228
peaches, caramelised,
    with spiced yogurt........225
pears with ricotta, date
    and maple filling...........225
pecans, roasted, herbed
    chicken kebabs with 88
pepper lamb steaks
    with tomato jam 118
peppered beef 164
peppered steak
    sandwich 137

pesto bread......................73
pesto butter 238
pesto fish kebabs..............56
pesto, capsicum, and
    mashed kumara,
    rib steaks with 162
pesto, coriander, chicken
    kebabs with 33
pesto, mint and pistachio,
    kebabs with 121
pesto, sun-dried tomato,
    lamb chops with 126
pilaf, kashmiri, chutney
    chicken breast with 77
pine nuts in
    lime vinaigrette,
    mesclun with 234
pineapple, caramelised,
    pork with 187
piquant grilled steaks.......141
pistachio pesto, mint
    and, kebabs with..........121
pizza, chorizo 132
pizza, roasted
    vegetable.....................132
pizza, satay prawn 133
pizza, three-mushroom.....133
plum crabs, chilli...............58
plum glaze, lamb with 116
pork and
    mandarin salad.............186
pork chutney burgers.......197
pork kebabs, hoisin..........184
pork kebabs,
    indian, with
    mango chutney 178
pork kebabs, spicy...........180
pork loin, salt-rubbed
    roasted, with sage........175
pork ribs, sticky...............179
pork spare ribs,
    american-style 14
pork with caramelised
    pineapple 187
pork, chinese
    marinated 176
pork, spiced, skewers,
    with honey glaze 174
port-smoked beef.............160
portuguese chicken 90
potato salad,
    german hot 232
potato skins 18
potato, jacket, mustard
    T-bone with 148
potatoes and mushrooms
    with olives 223
potatoes in foil,
    barbecued....................238
potatoes with aïoli............212
potatoes, greek lamb
    with lemon and 114
prawn kebabs with
    chilli lime sauce.............29
prawn kebabs, chilli,
    black bean and 34
prawn, satay, pizza 133

prawns, basil, with
avocado mash..............20

prawns, coconut, with
turmeric coriander
mayonnaise..................45

prawns, garlic.....................32

prawns, salt and pepper....24

pumpkin with
walnut dressing...........220

puree, green pea, lemon
pepper cutlets with.......112

quail, sweet-and-spicy......84

red onion and
balsamic jam.................206

red wine marinade...........170

relish, tomato,
sausages with...............194

rib steaks with
capsicum pesto and
mashed kumara.........162

ribs, american-style
pork spare.......................14

ribs, honey
mustard glazed............183

ribs, sticky pork...............179

ribs, sweet chilli beef.......142

ribs, tex-mex...................182

rice, nutty, snapper...........61

ricotta, date and maple
filling, pears with..........225

roast leg of lamb with garlic
and rosemary...............120

roast vegetables
with herb and
garlic dressing...........222

roasted vegetable pizza...132

rosemary chicken,
mustard..........................81

rosemary smoked lamb,
garlic and......................122

rosemary, roast leg of lamb
with garlic and..............120

sage, salt-rubbed roasted
pork loin with...............175

salad, baby rocket
and parmesan..............233

salad, chickpea
and tomato, veal
chops with..................144

salad, chickpea, lamb
chermoulla with............117

salad, cucumber,
tandoori lamb
cutlets with.................125

salad, cucumber, thai-style
steaks with...................146

salad, german
hot potato....................232

salad, mandarin,
pork and......................186

salad, pasta.....................228

salad, sliced tomato,
basil and red onion.....236

salad, thai-beef...............161

salad, three-bean............230

salad, tomato chickpea,
grilled curried
cutlets with.................129

salad, watercress,
squid with......................48

salsa, avocado
and tomato...................238

salsa, avocado, cajun
seafood kebabs with......64

salsa, capsicum,
steaks with...................140

salsa, lentil,
chicken with.................100

salsa, olive, tuna with........42

salsa, tomato.....................37

salsa, tomato and
onion, lime-marinated
cutlets with...................46

salsa, tomato and onion,
veal souvlakia with.......138

salsa, tomato, lamb
burgers with.................202

salt and pepper prawns.....24

salt-rubbed roasted pork
loin with sage..............175

sandwich, peppered
steak............................137

sandwiches, open,
steak and aïoli.............158

satay prawn pizza............133

satay, chicken....................80

sauce, chilli lime,
prawn kebabs with........29

sauce, coriander
chilli, cumin fish
cutlets with...................66

sausage and caramelised
onion hot dogs.............193

sausages with
tomato relish................194

sausages, beef,
with onion....................200

sausages, lamb
and burghul.................196

seafood kebabs, cajun,
with avocado salsa........64

seasoning, couscous,
lemon rosemary
chicken with..................96

sesame chicken cutlets......89

sesame lamb....................113

skewers, beef, on
lettuce cups.................136

skewers, bombay-
spiced chicken...............92

skewers, lemon grass,
chicken on......................94

skewers, spiced pork,
with honey glaze..........174

sliced tomato, basil
and red onion salad.....236

snapper, nutty rice............61

sour cream with sweet
chilli sauce...................239

souvlakia, lamb................106

souvlakia, veal,
with tomato and
onion salsa.................138

soy and chilli
fish parcels....................60

spareribs, beef................157

spatchcock, indian,
with green chilli
and coriander................82

spatchcocks, middle
eastern spicy roasted.....98

spiced pork skewers
with honey glaze..........174

spiced trout with
cucumber and yogurt.....69

spicy pork kebabs...........180

spicy veal cutlets.............150

spinach and
fetta damper..................72

squid with
watercress salad............48

squid, devilled, with
lime vinaigrette..............13

steak and aïoli
open sandwiches.........158

steak towers,
mediterranean..............166

steak with
herb vinaigrette...........169

steak, peppered,
sandwich......................137

steaks with
capsicum salsa............140

steaks, fish with tomato
and chilli butter.............57

steaks, herbed lamb........128

steaks, pepper lamb,
with tomato jam............118

steaks, piquant grilled......141

steaks, rib, with
capsicum pesto
and mashed kumara..162

steaks, thai-style, with
cucumber salad...........146

sticky pork ribs................179

sweet chilli beef ribs........142

sweet chilli
chicken drumsticks........76

sweet chilli dip...................37

sweet chilli lime fish..........70

sweet chilli sauce,
sour cream with...........239

sweet-and-spicy quail........84

swordfish with
olive paste.....................62

tabbouleh.........................237

tandoori beef with
grilled limes.................149

tandoori drumsticks............78

tandoori lamb cutlets
with cucumber salad....125

tandoori lamb naan..........109

tapenade, olive,
and mozzarella
turkish bread.................72

T-bone, mustard, with
jacket potato................148

teriyaki beef kebabs.........152

tex-mex ribs.....................182

thai-beef salad................161

thai-style fish cutlets..........52

thai-style steaks with
cucumber salad...........146

three-bean salad..............230

three-mushroom pizza......133

thyme chicken with
grilled citrus....................85

tomato relish,
sausages with...............194

tomato salsa.......................37

tomato salsa, lamb
burgers with.................202

tomato, sliced, basil
and red onion salad.....236

tomatoes with
walnut gremolata..........211

trout, ocean, grilled
lime and pepper.............65

trout, spiced, with
cucumber and yogurt.....69

tuna with char-grilled
vegetables......................49

tuna with olive salsa..........42

turkey with lime
and mustard...................86

turkey, marjoram
and orange.....................97

tzatziki, beetroot................36

veal chops with
chickpea and
tomato salad...............144

veal cutlets in
maple marinade...........156

veal cutlets, spicy............150

veal roll-up.......................168

veal souvlakia with tomato
and onion salsa............138

vegetable, roasted,
pizza............................132

vegetables with
haloumi........................218

vegetables, char-grilled,
tuna with........................49

vegetables, garlic
and rosemary...............216

vegetables, roast,
with herb and
garlic dressing...........222

vinaigrette, lime, devilled
squid with......................13

vinaigrette, lime, mesclun
with pine nuts in...........234

vinaigrette, steak
with herb......................169

walnut dressing,
pumpkin with...............220

walnut gremolata,
tomatoes with...............211

watercress salad,
squid with......................48

wings, marinated
chicken...........................26

yogurt and ginger,
barramundi with.............40

yogurt marinade...............171

yogurt, spiced trout with
cucumber and................69

yogurt, spiced,
caramelised
peaches with...............225

zucchini with
chermoulla dressing.....215

facts and figures

Wherever you live, you'll be able to use our recipes with the help of these easy-to-follow conversions. While these conversions are approximate only, the difference between an exact and the approximate conversion of various liquid and dry measures is but minimal and will not affect your cooking results.

dry measures

metric	imperial
15g	1/2oz
30g	1oz
60g	2oz
90g	3oz
125g	4oz (1/4lb)
155g	5oz
185g	6oz
220g	7oz
250g	8oz (1/2lb)
280g	9oz
315g	10oz
345g	11oz
375g	12oz (3/4lb)
410g	13oz
440g	14oz
470g	15oz
500g	16oz (1lb)
750g	24oz (11/2lb)
1kg	32oz (2lb)

liquid measures

metric	imperial
30ml	1 fluid oz
60ml	2 fluid oz
100ml	3 fluid oz
125ml	4 fluid oz
150ml	5 fluid oz (1/4 pint/1 gill)
190ml	6 fluid oz
250ml	8 fluid oz
300ml	10 fluid oz (1/2 pint)
500ml	16 fluid oz
600ml	20 fluid oz (1 pint)
1000ml (1 litre)	13/4 pints

helpful measures

metric	imperial
3mm	1/8in
6mm	1/4in
1cm	1/2in
2cm	3/4in
2.5cm	1in
5cm	2in
6cm	21/2in
8cm	3in
10cm	4in
13cm	5in
15cm	6in
18cm	7in
20cm	8in
23cm	9in
25cm	10in
28cm	11in
30cm	12in (1ft)

measuring equipment

The difference between one country's measuring cups and another's is, at most, within a 2 or 3 teaspoon variance. (For the record, 1 Australian metric measuring cup holds approximately 250ml.) The most accurate way of measuring dry ingredients is to weigh them. When measuring liquids, use a clear glass or plastic jug with the metric markings. (One Australian metric tablespoon holds 20ml; one Australian metric teaspoon holds 5ml.)

Note: North America, NZ and the UK use 15ml tablespoons. All cup and spoon measurements are level.

We use large eggs having an average weight of 60g.

how to measure

When using graduated metric measuring cups, shake dry ingredients loosely into the appropriate cup. Do not tap the cup on a bench or tightly pack the ingredients unless directed to do so. Level top of measuring cups and measuring spoons with a knife. When measuring liquids, place a clear glass or plastic jug with metric markings on a flat surface to check accuracy at eye level.

oven temperatures

These oven temperatures are only a guide. Always check the manufacturer's manual.

	°C (Celsius)	°F (Fahrenheit)	Gas Mark
Very slow	120	250	1
Slow	150	300	2
Moderately slow	160	325	3
Moderate	180 - 190	350 - 375	4
Moderately hot	200 - 210	400 - 425	5
Hot	220 - 230	450 - 475	6
Very hot	240 - 250	500 - 525	7

Editor *Deborah Quick*
Designer *Caryl Wiggins*
Food editor *Louise Patniotis*
Special feature photographer *Scott Cameron*
Special feature stylist *Cherise Koch*
Special feature home economist *Alison Webb*

Test Kitchen Staff
Food director *Pamela Clark*
Test kitchen manager *Kimberley Coverdale*
Senior home economist *Kellie Ann*
Home economists *Emma Braz, Kelly Cruickshanks,*
Sarah Hobbs, Amanda Kelly, Naomi Scesny, Alison Webb
Editorial coordinator *Amanda Josling*
Kitchen assistants *Vassa Karpathiou, Aileen Rosas*

ACP Books Staff
Editorial director *Susan Tomnay*
Creative director *Hieu Nguyen*
Senior editors *Julie Collard, Liz Neate*
Senior writer and editor *Lynda Wilton*
Editor *Deborah Quick*
Designers *Mary Keep, Caryl Wiggins, Alison Windmill*
Studio manager *Caryl Wiggins*
Editorial coordinator *Holly van Oyen*
Editorial assistant *Lana Meldrum*
Publishing manager (sales) *Jennifer McDonald*
Publishing manager (rights & new projects) *Jane Hazell*
Assistant brand manager *Donna Gianniotis*

Pre-press *Harry Palmer*
Production manager *Carol Currie*
Business manager *Sally Lees*

Chief executive officer *John Alexander*
Group publisher *Jill Baker*
Publisher *Sue Wannan*

Produced by *ACP books*, Sydney.
Printing by Dai Nippon in Hong Kong.
Published by ACP Publishing Pty Limited,
54 Park St, Sydney; GPO Box 4088, Sydney, NSW 1028.
Ph: (02) 9282 8618 Fax: (02) 9267 9438.
acpbooks@acp.com.au
www.acpbooks.com.au

To order books phone 136 116.
Send recipe enquiries to
reccipeenquiries@acp.com.au

AUSTRALIA: Distributed by Network Services,
GPO Box 4088, Sydney, NSW 1028.
Ph: (02) 9282 8777 Fax: (02) 9264 3278.
UNITED KINGDOM: Distributed by Australian
Consolidated Press (UK), Moulton Park Business Centre,
Red House Rd, Moulton Park, Northampton, NN3 6AQ
Ph: (01604) 497 531 Fax: (01604) 497 533
acpukltd@aol.com
CANADA: Distributed by Whitecap Books Ltd, 351 Lynn Ave,
North Vancouver, BC, V7J 2C4, Ph: (604) 980 9852.
NEW ZEALAND: Distributed by Netlink Distribution
Company, Level 4, 23 Hargreaves St, College Hill,
Auckland 1, Ph: (9) 302 7616.
SOUTH AFRICA: Distributed by PSD Promotions (Pty) Ltd,
PO Box 1175, Isando 1600, SA, Ph: (011) 392 6065

Great Barbecue Food
Includes index.
ISBN 1 86396 262 X

1. Barbecue cookery . I. Title: Great barbecue food
II. Title: Australian Women's Weekly.
641.76

The publishers would like to thank
Barbeques Galore **for generously supplying**
the barbecues and props used in this book.

Photographers: *Alan Benson, Scott Cameron,*
Robert Clark, Brett Danton, Joe Filshie,
Rowan Fotheringham, Ashley Mackevicius,
Andre Martin, Valerie Martin, Stuart Scott,
Rob Shaw, Brett Stevens, Robert Taylor

Stylists: *Frances Abdallaoui, Wendy Berecry,*
Marie-Helene Clauzon, Georgina Dolling, Kay Francis,
Jane Hann, Trish Heagerty, Cherise Koch,
Michelle Noerianto, Sarah O'Brien, Sophia Young

Cover: Teriyaki beef kebabs, page 152
Photographer: Scott Cameron
Stylist: Cherise Koch

Back cover: Honey mustard glazed ribs, page 183
Photographer: Scott Cameron
Stylist: Cherise Koch